Amateur photographer Janice F. Lowrance presents this collection of 50 beautiful pictures from Western Oklahoma, with Quarts Mountain Lodge areas featured, including Lake Altus-Lugert.

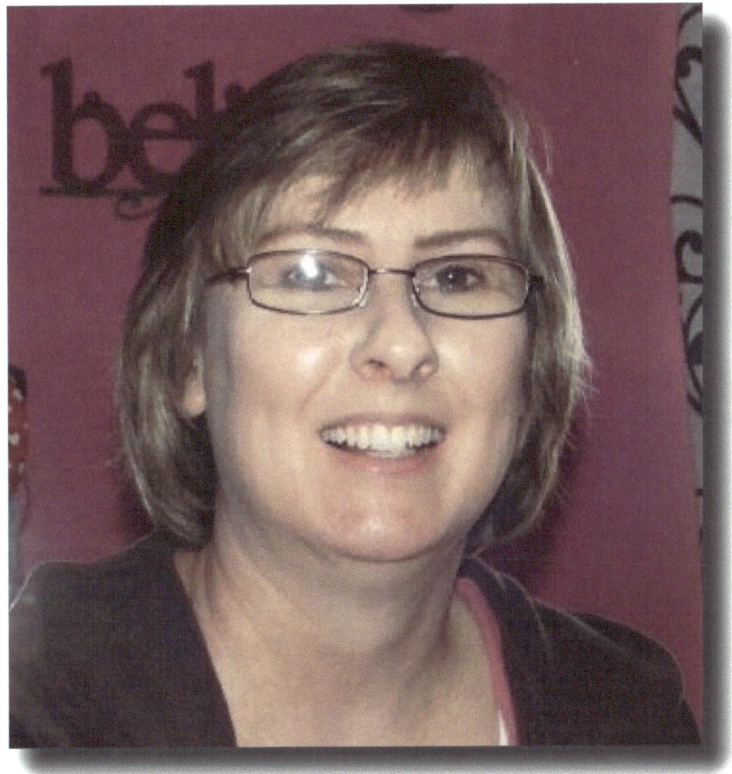

Copyright 2016 by: Janice F. Lowrance

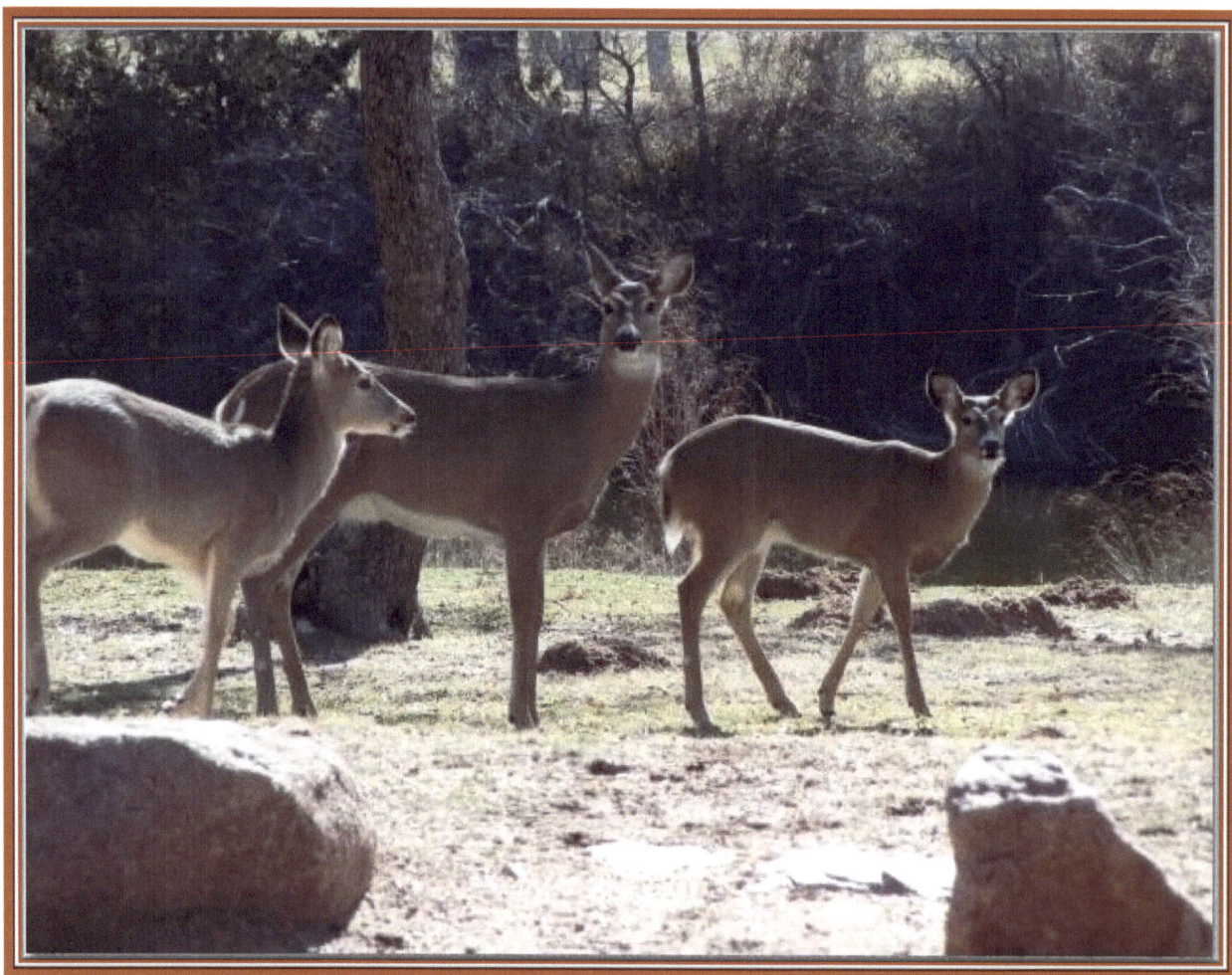

Beautiful Scenic Oklahoma in Photos

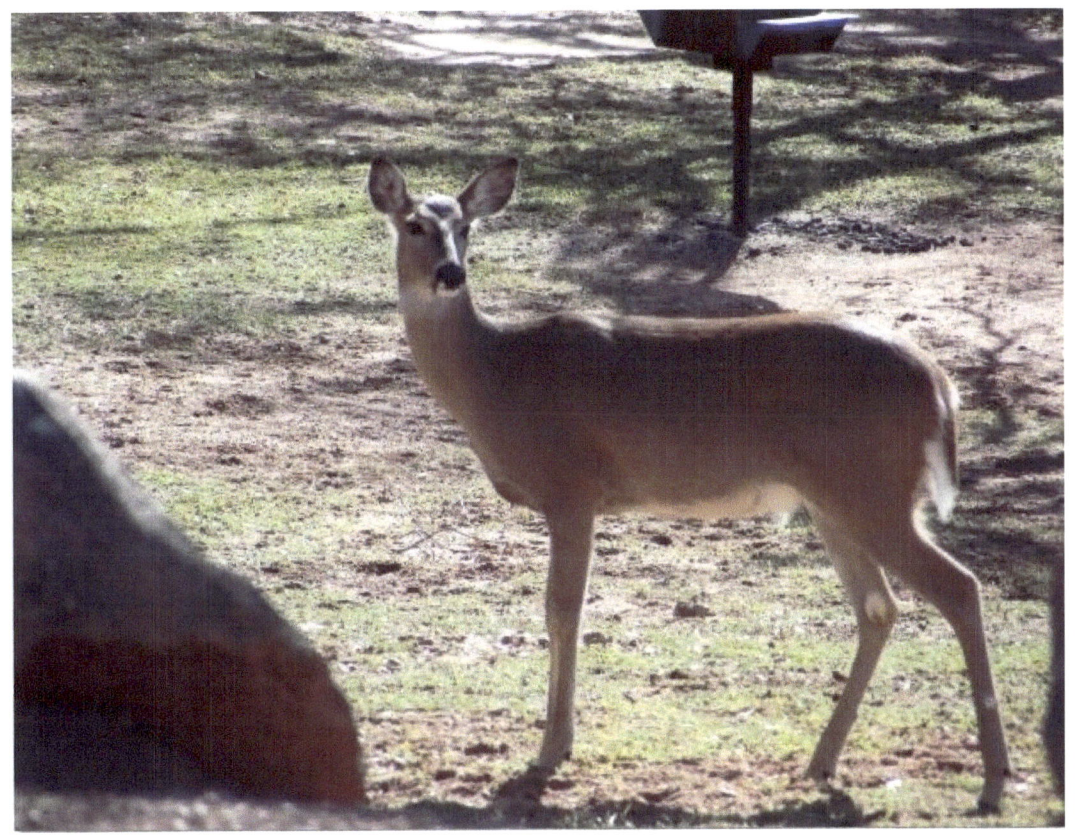

Beautiful Scenic Oklahoma in Photos

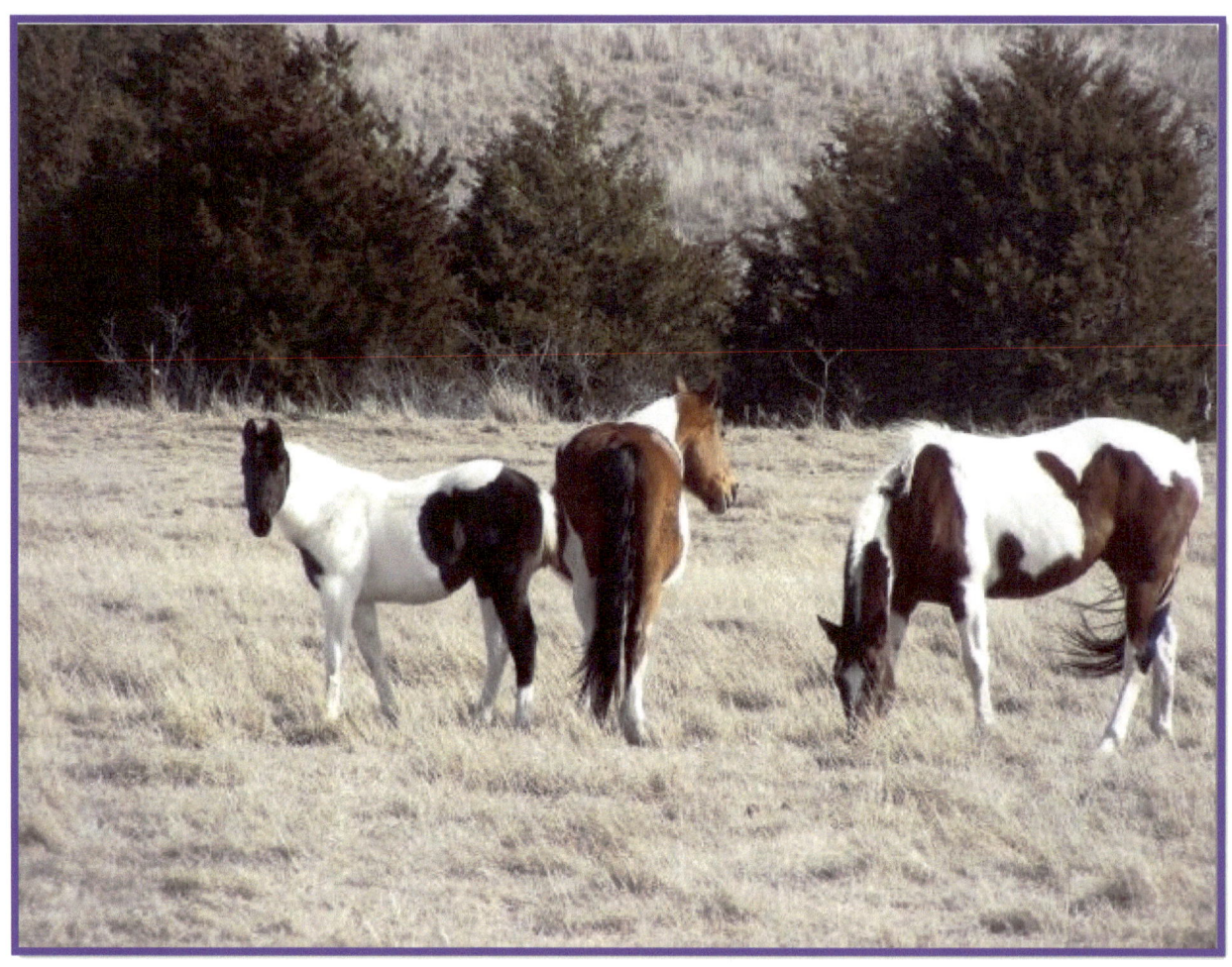

Beautiful Scenic Oklahoma in Photos

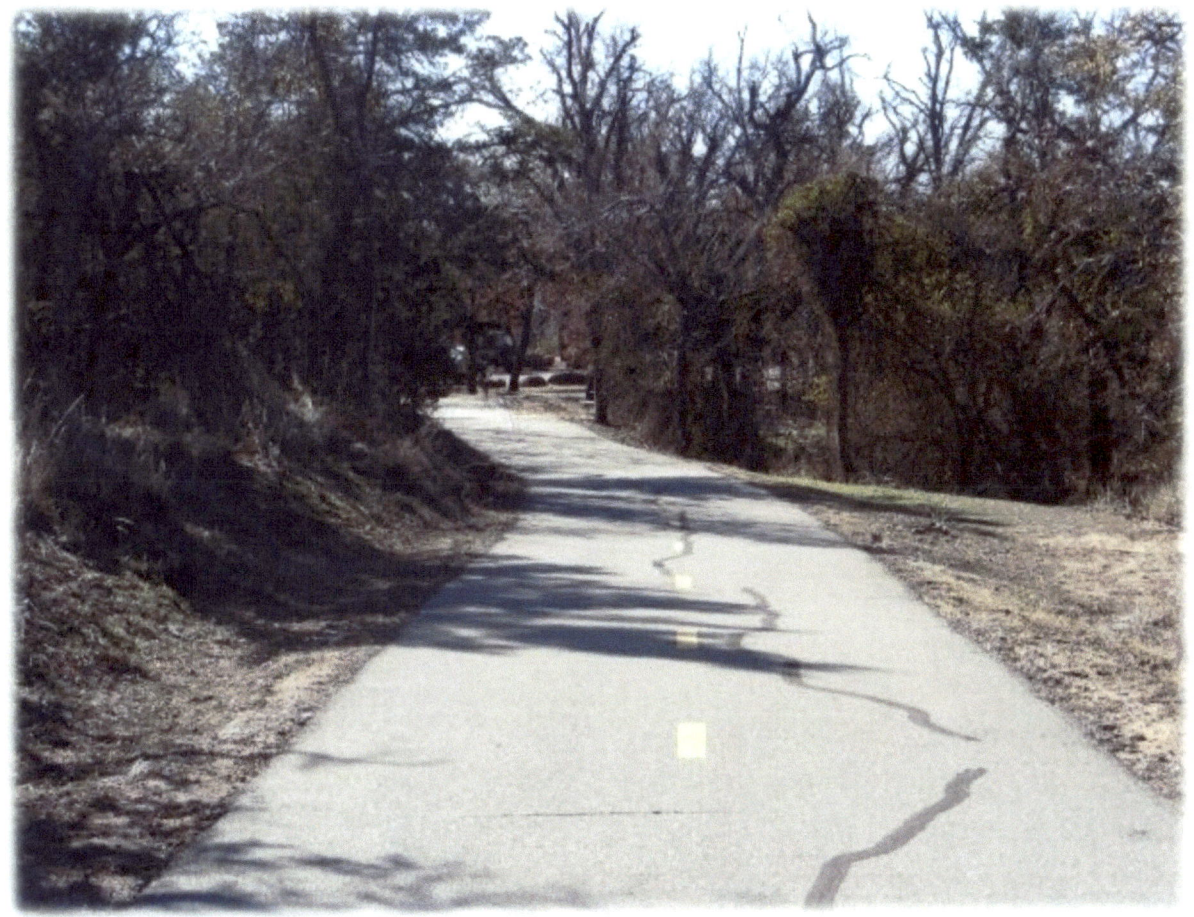

Beautiful Scenic Oklahoma in Photos

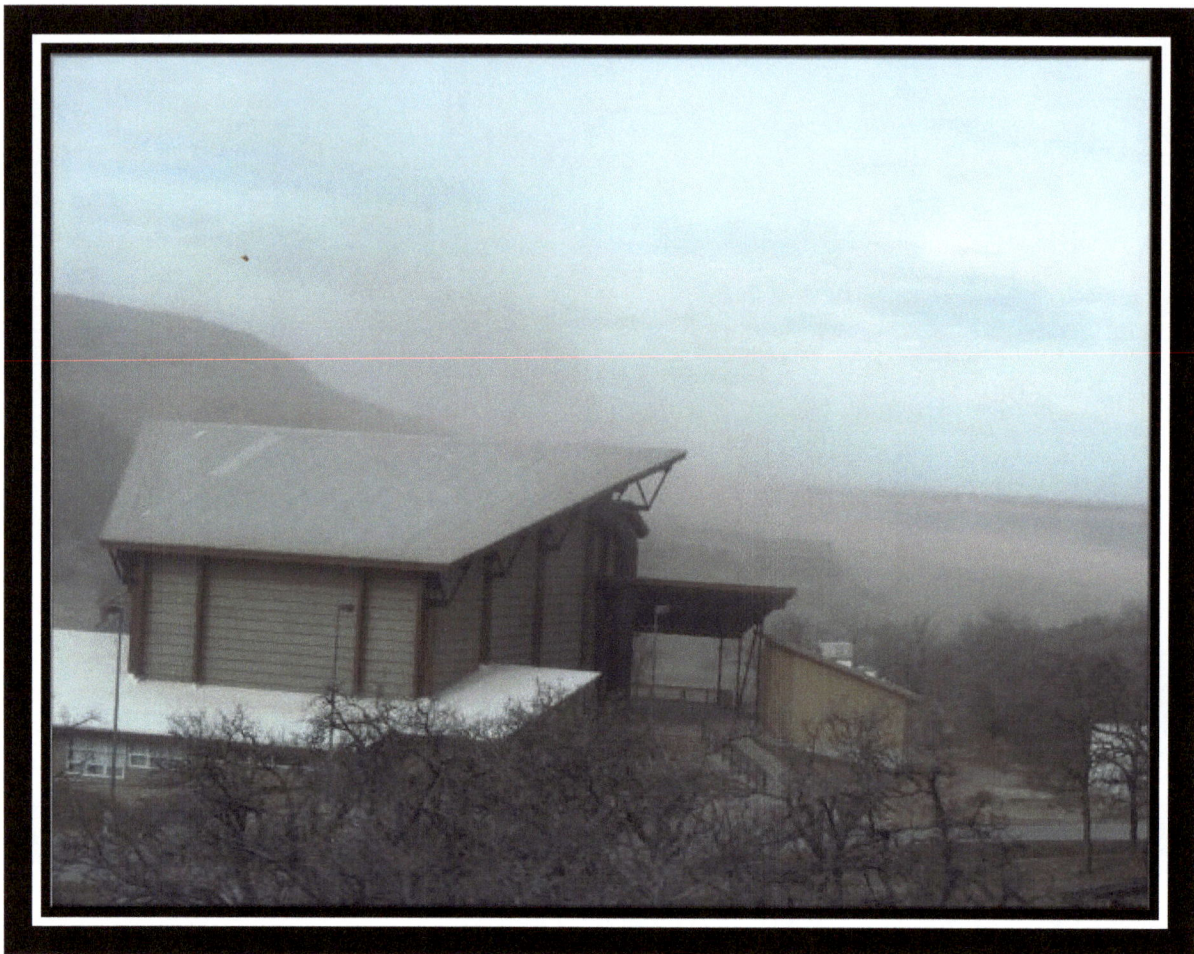

Beautiful Scenic Oklahoma in Photos

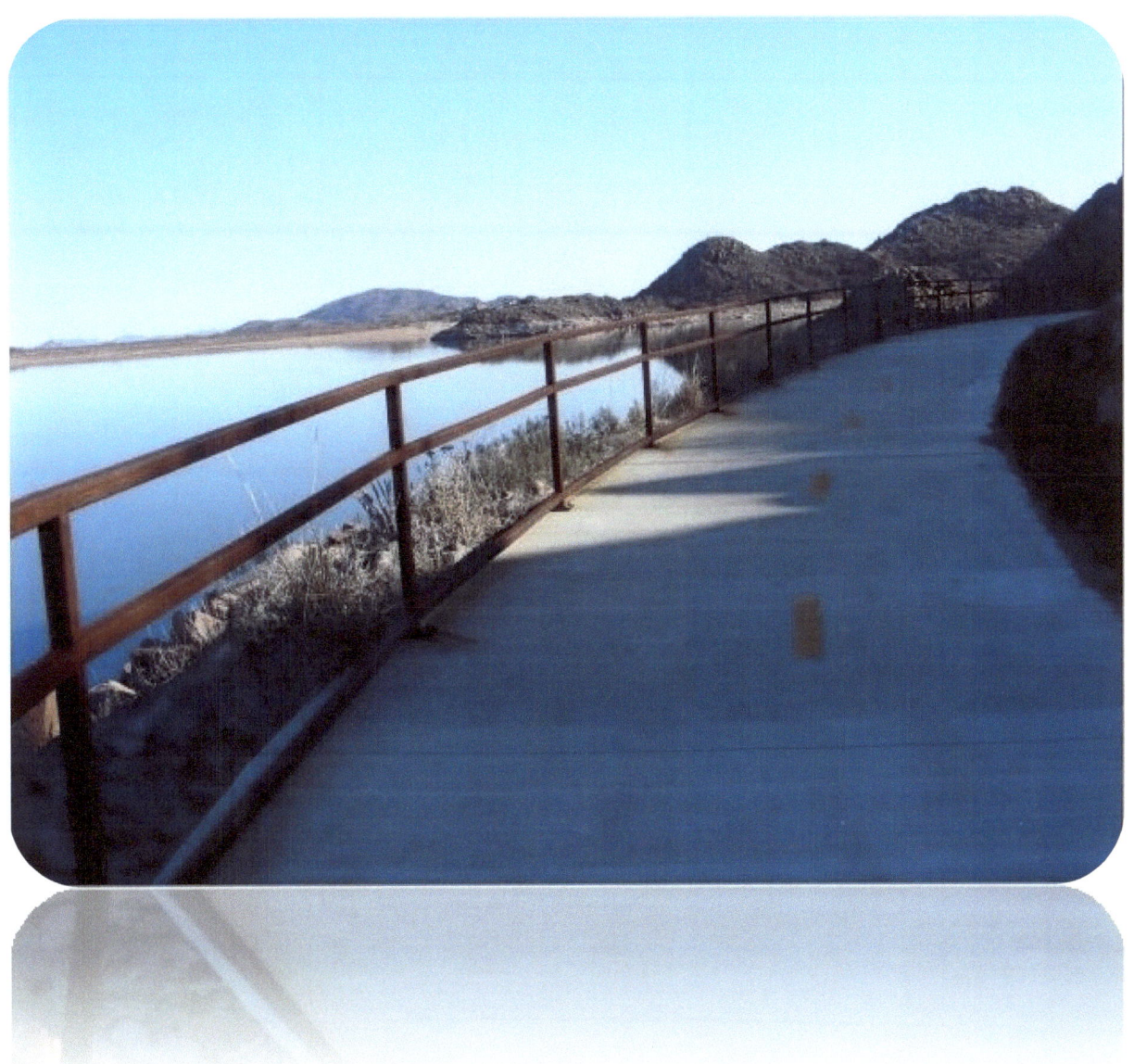

Beautiful Scenic Oklahoma in Photos

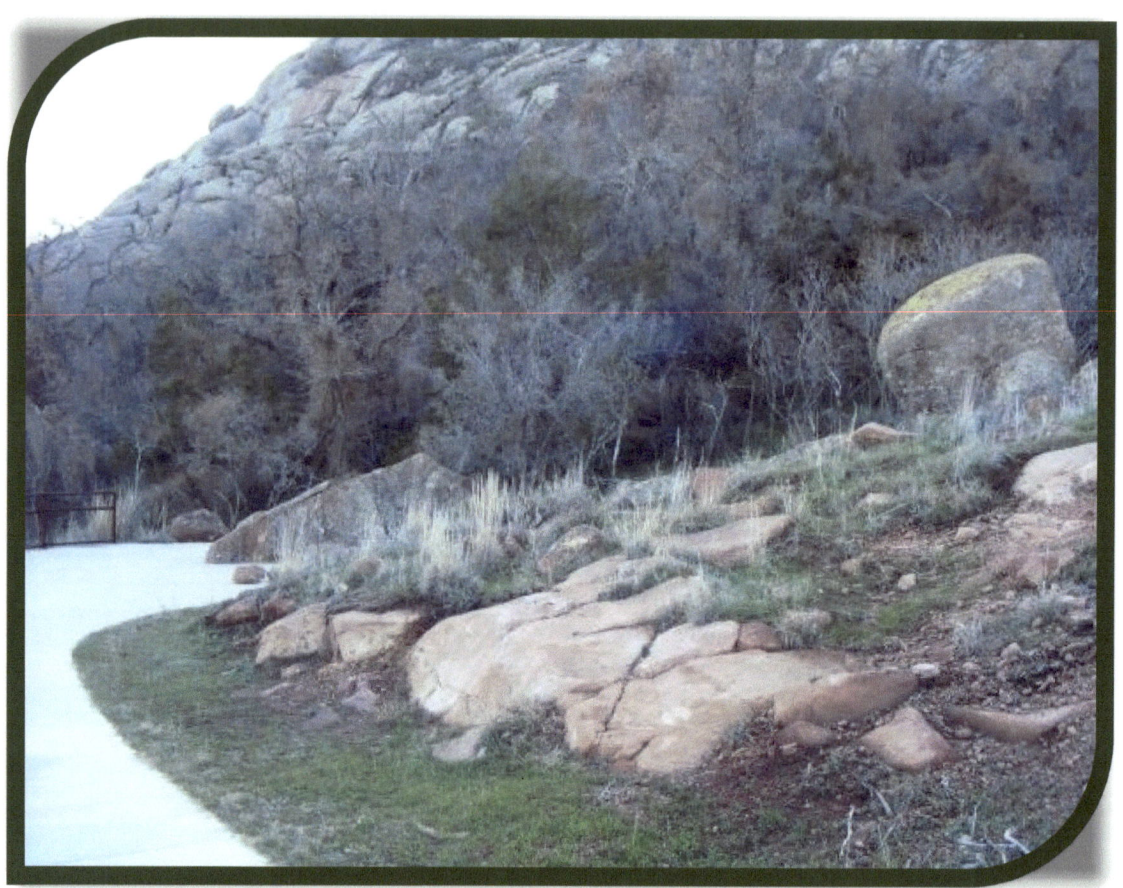

Beautiful Scenic Oklahoma in Photos

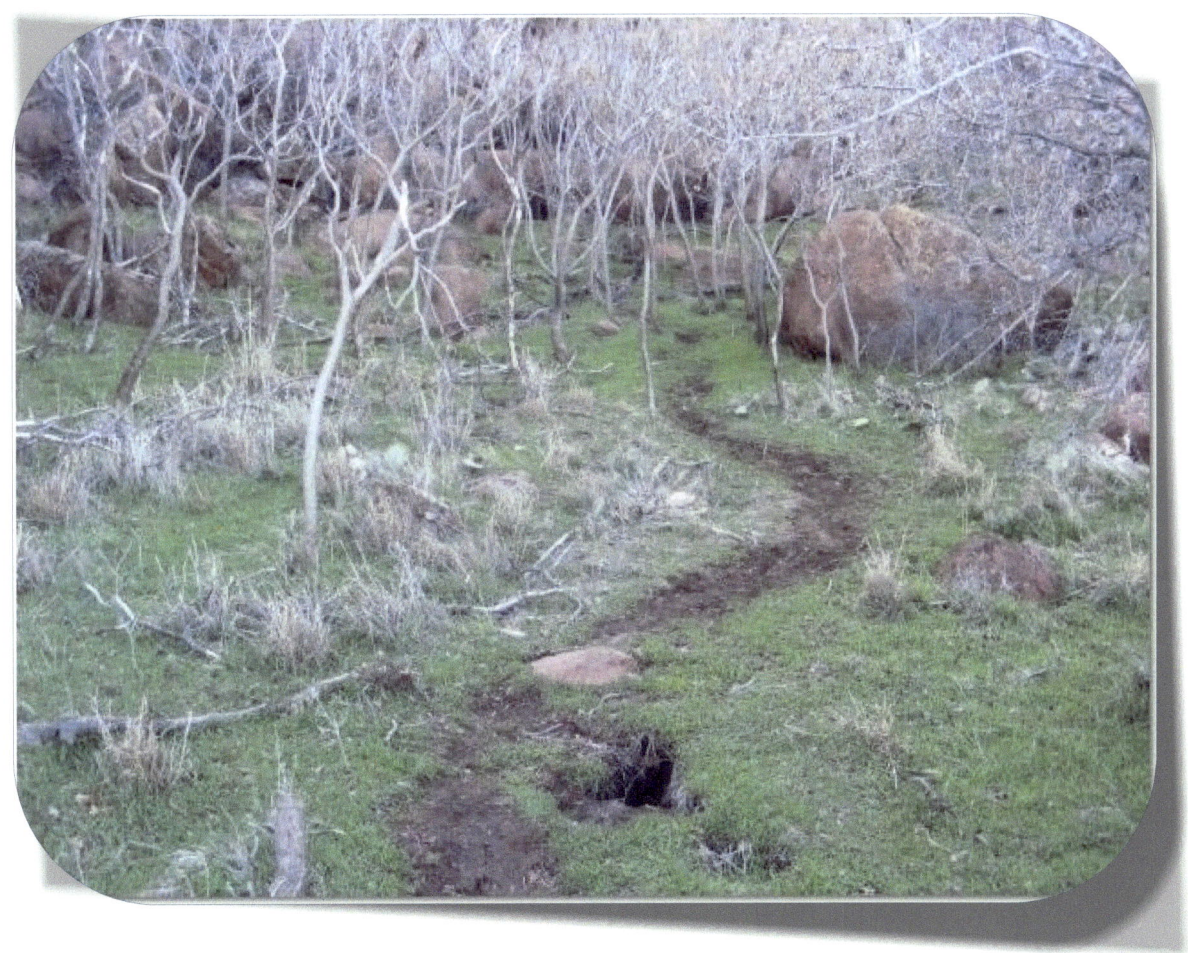

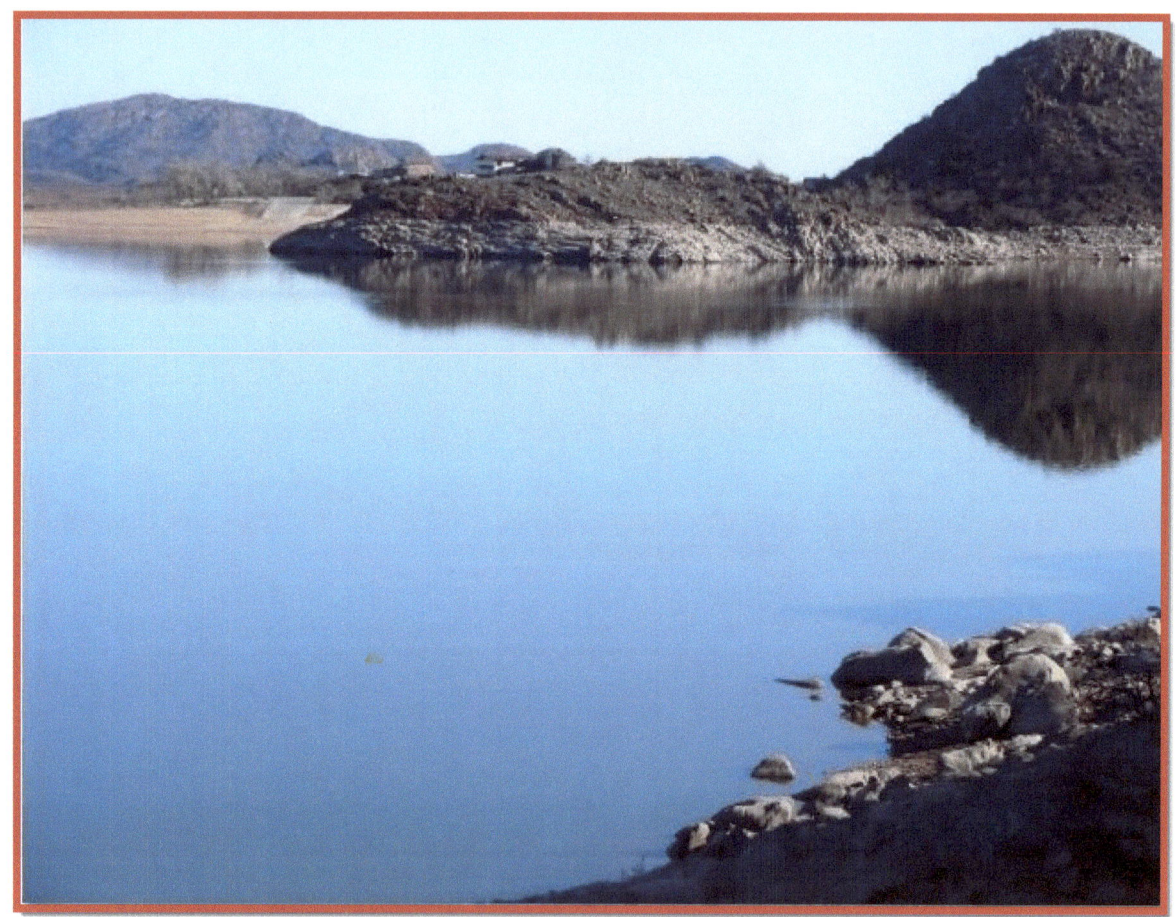

Beautiful Scenic Oklahoma in Photos

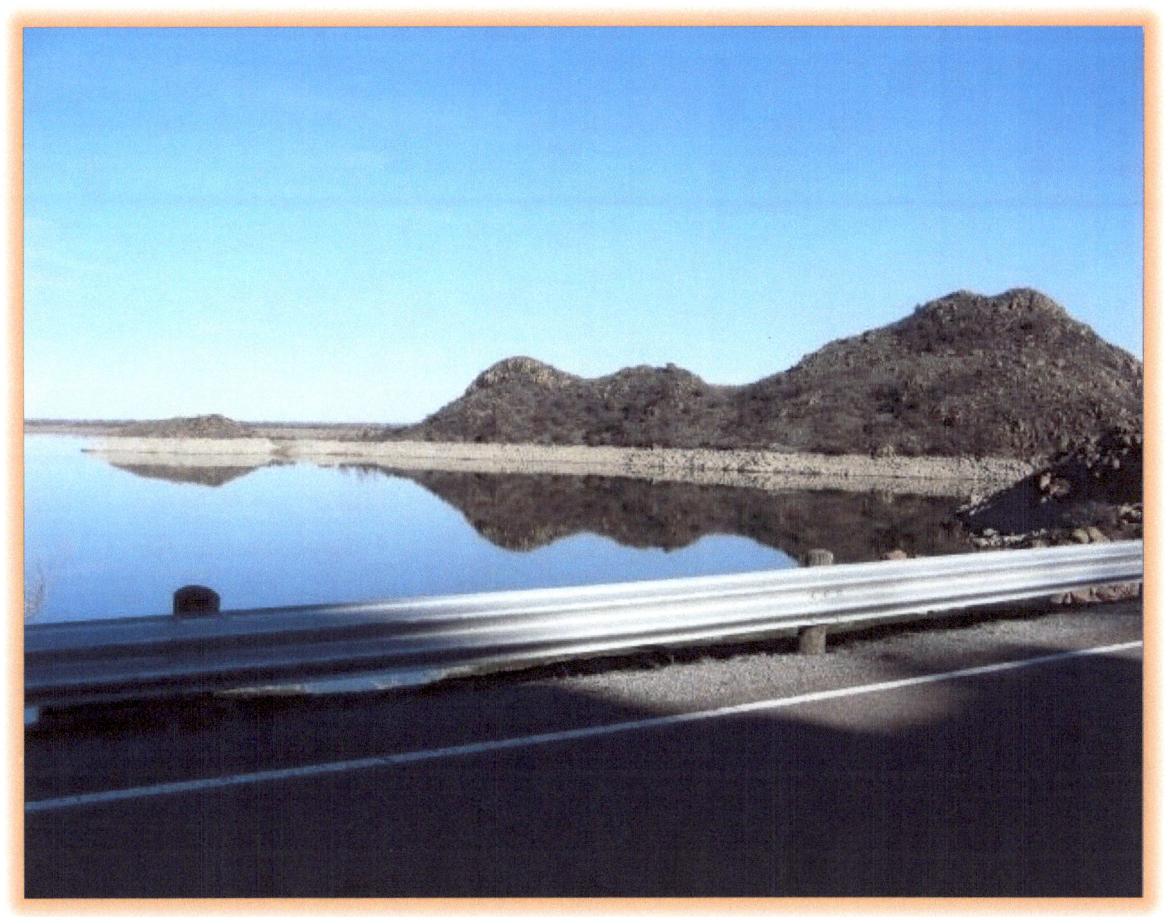

Beautiful Scenic Oklahoma in Photos

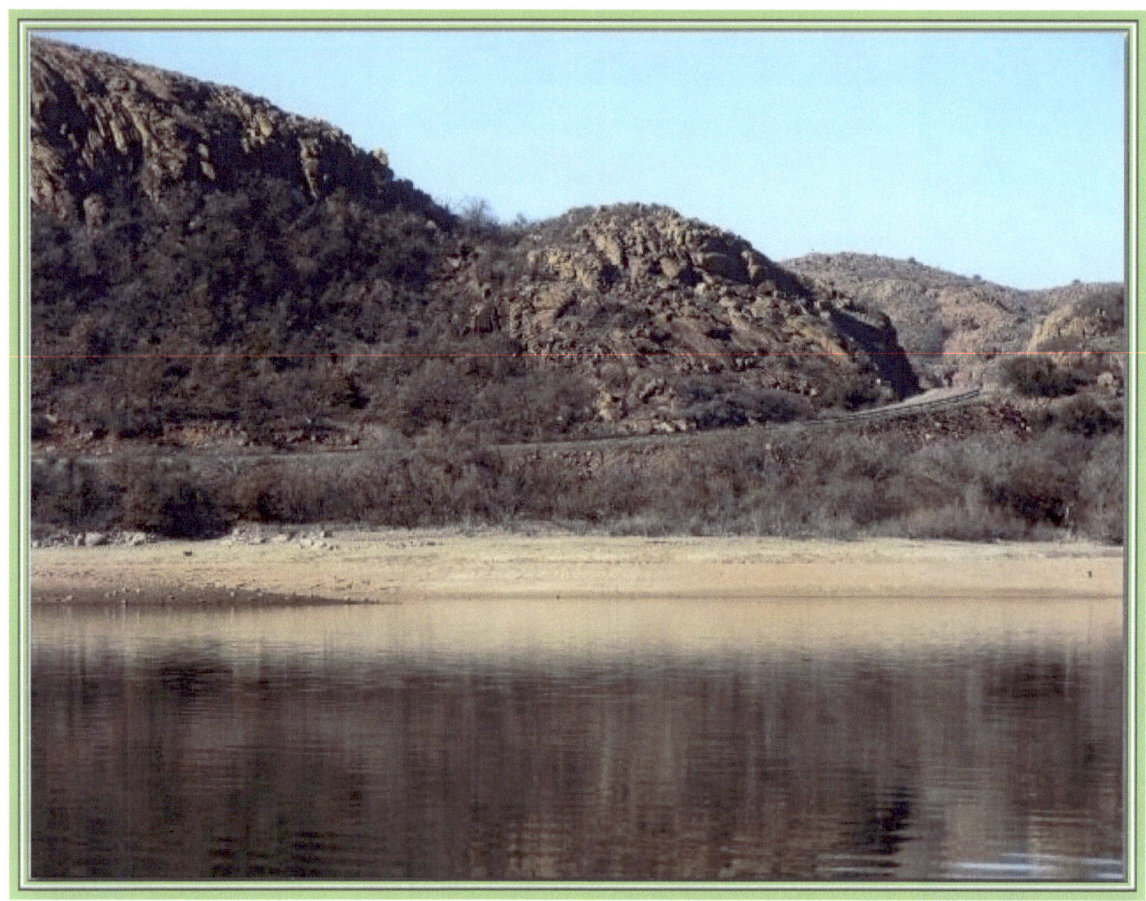

Beautiful Scenic Oklahoma in Photos

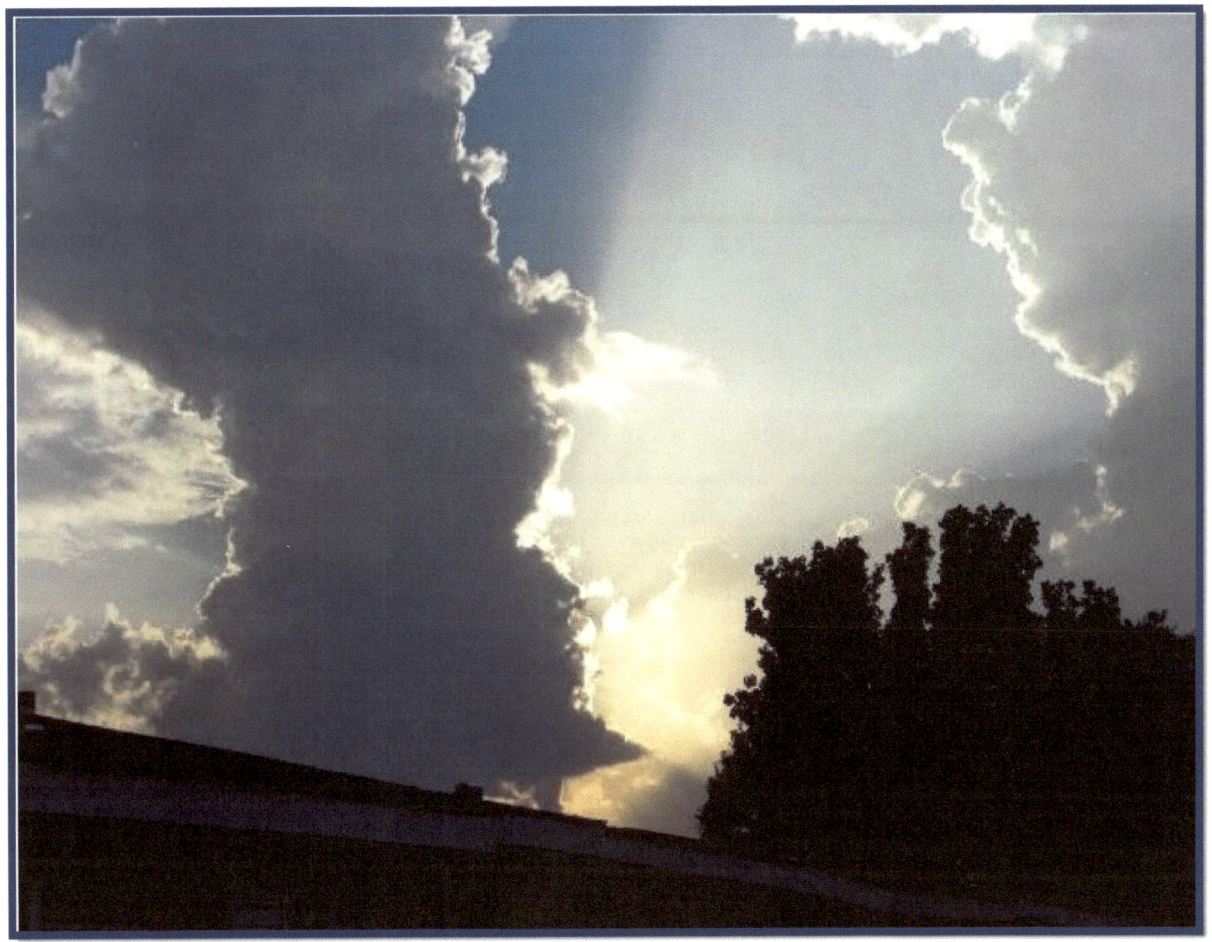

Beautiful Scenic Oklahoma in Photos

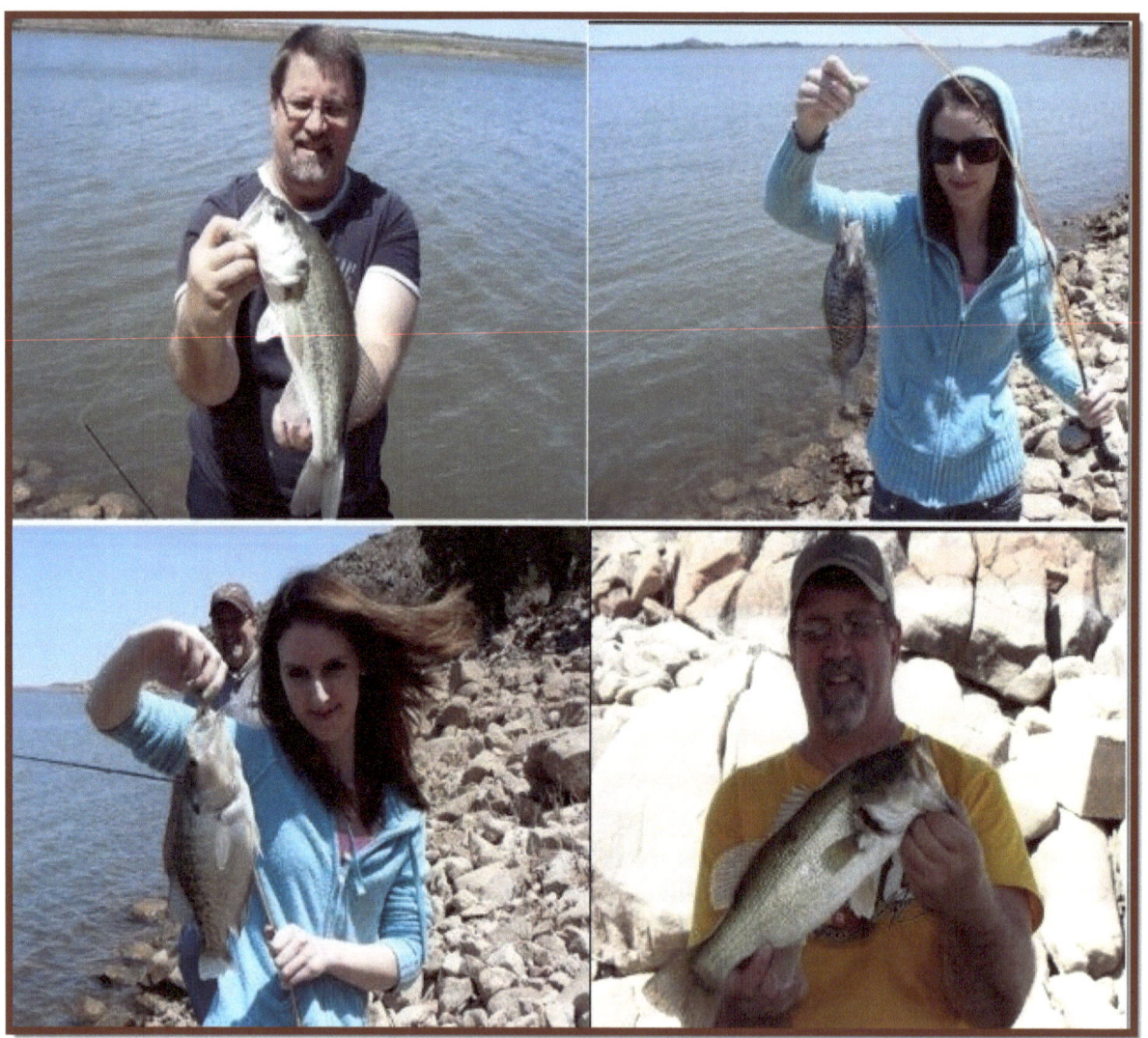

Beautiful Scenic Oklahoma in Photos

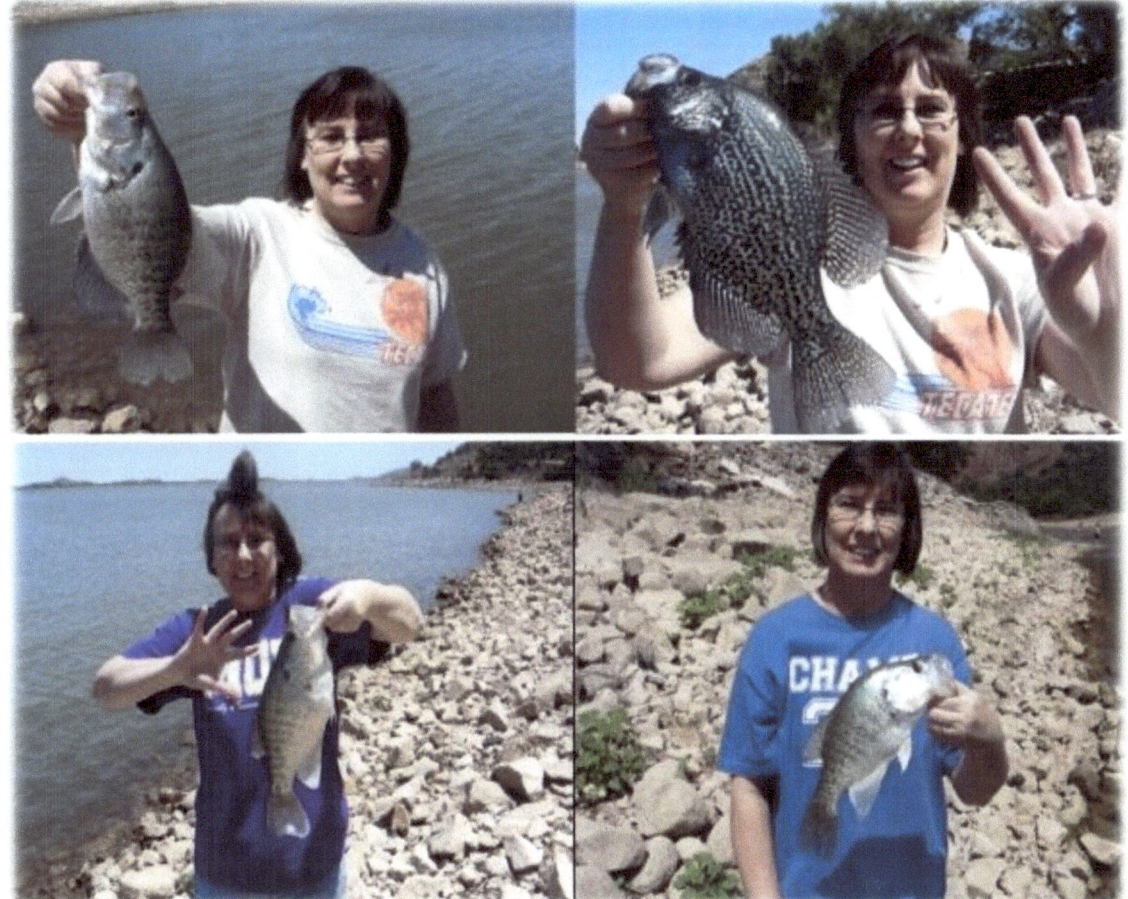

Beautiful Scenic Oklahoma in Photos

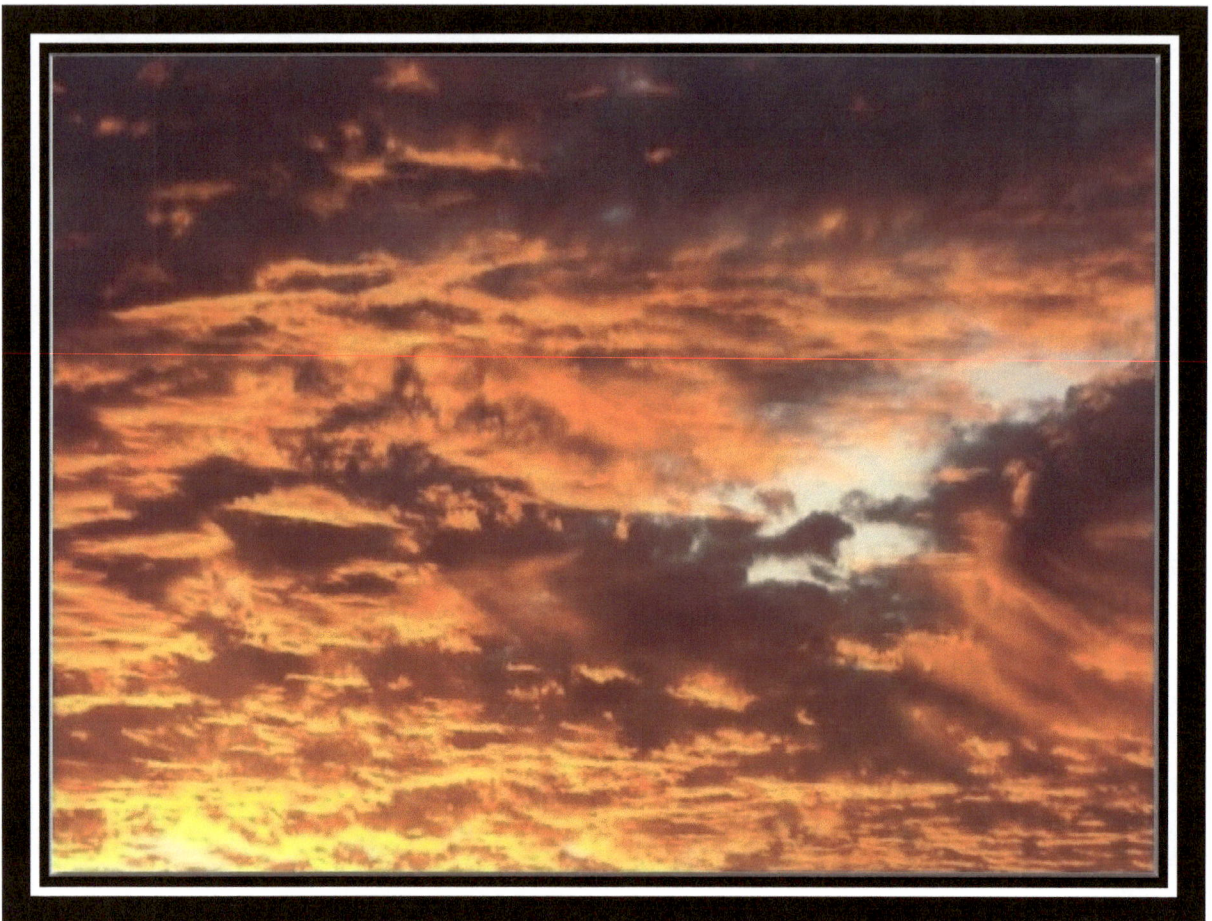

Beautiful Scenic Oklahoma in Photos

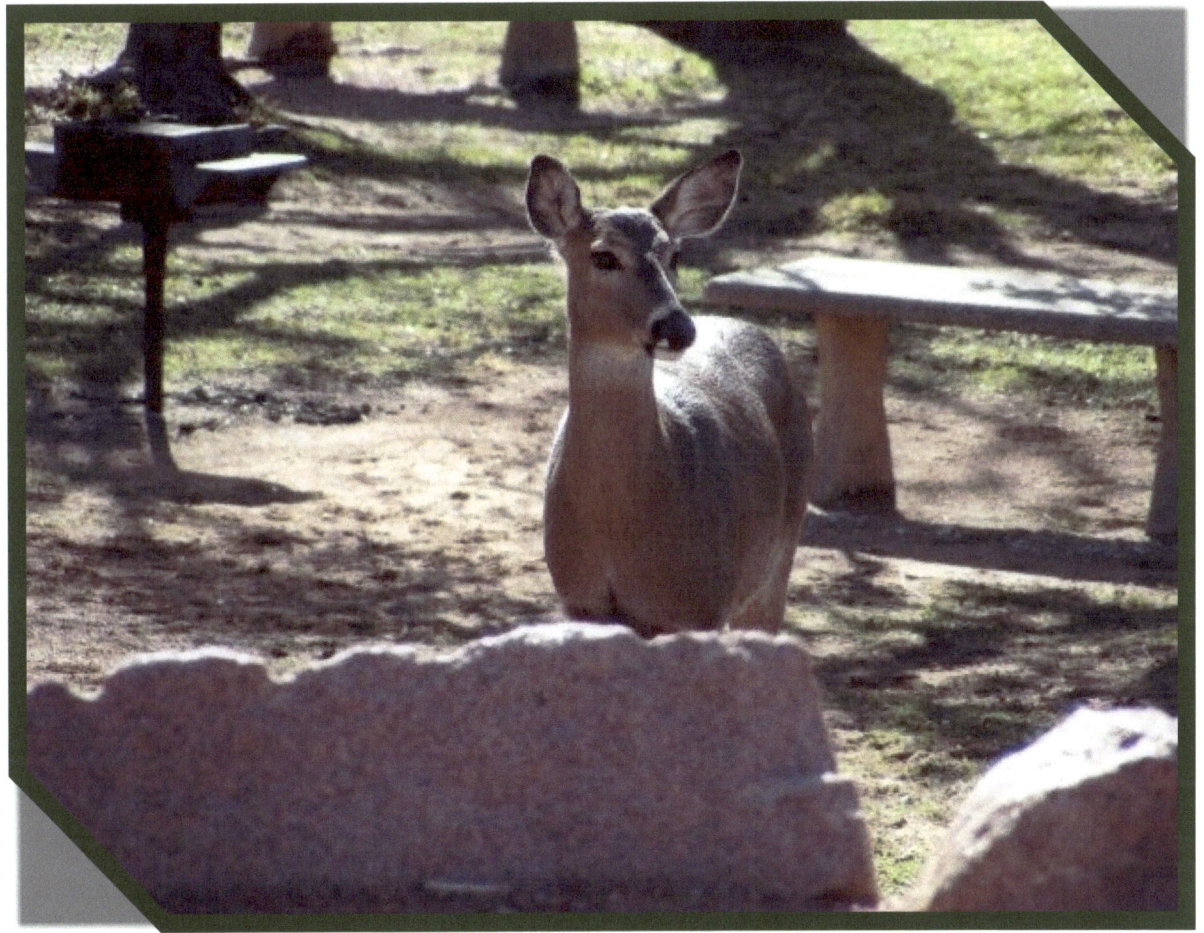

Beautiful Scenic Oklahoma in Photos

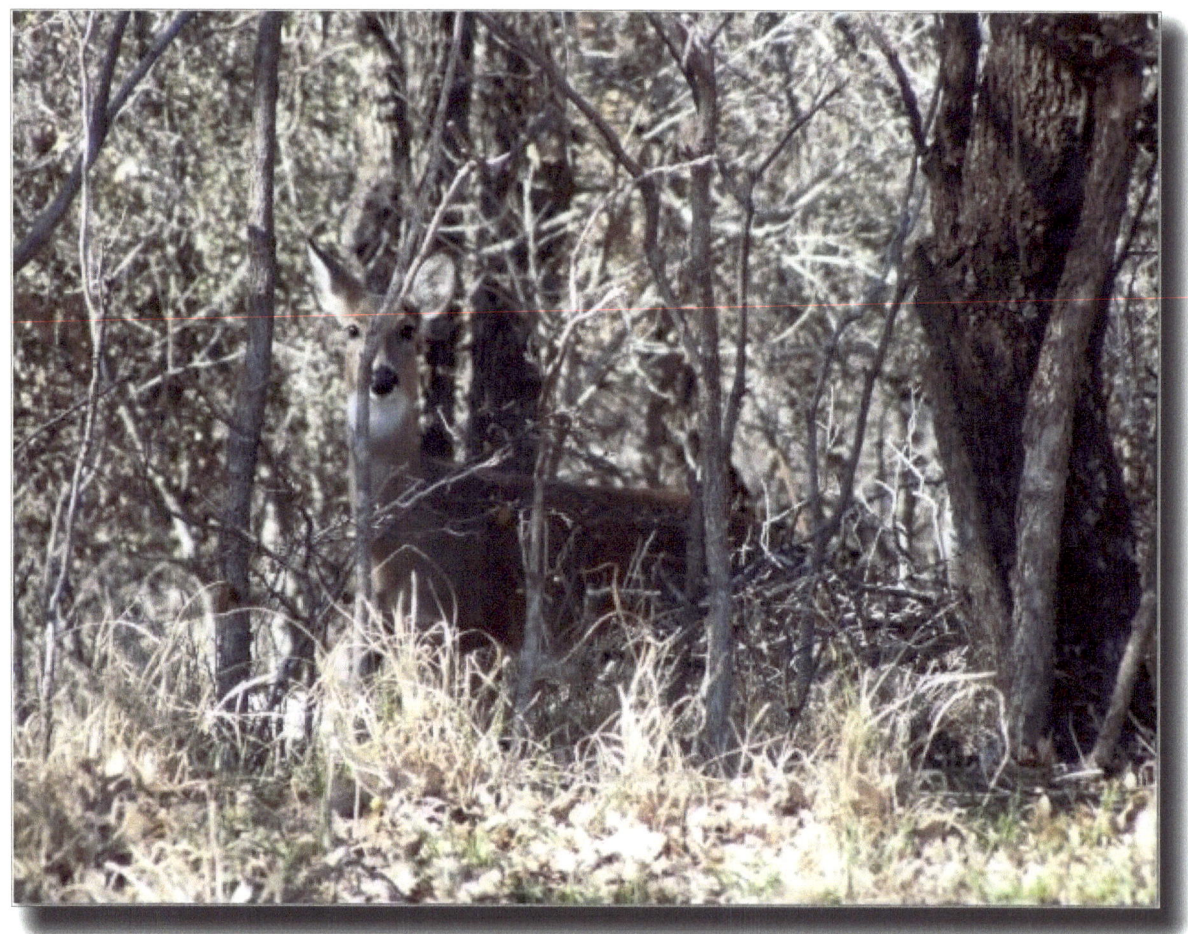

Beautiful Scenic Oklahoma in Photos

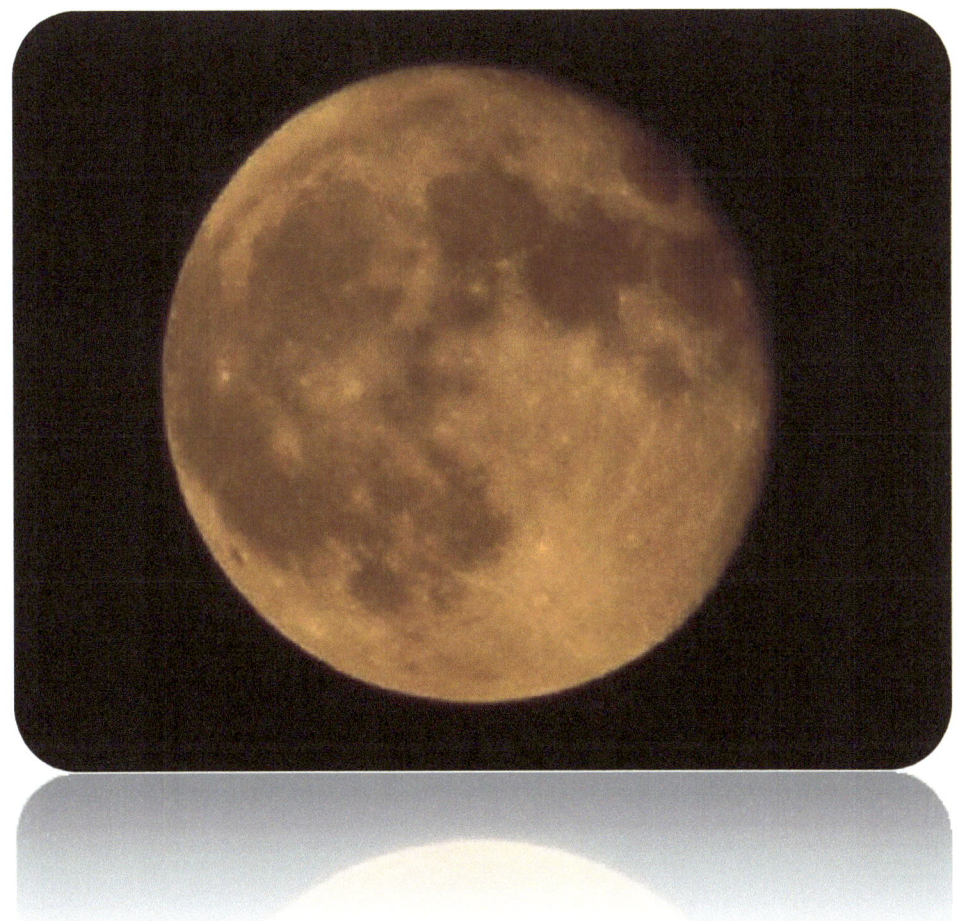

Beautiful Scenic Oklahoma in Photos

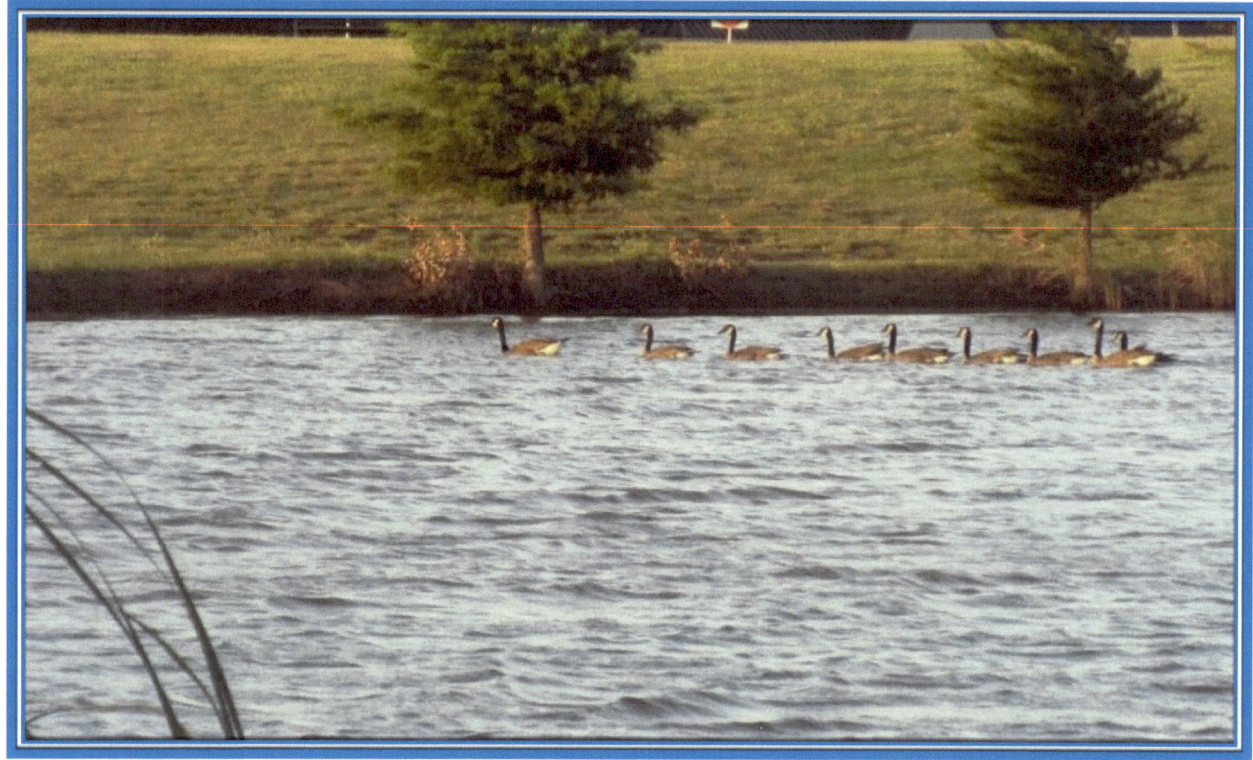

Beautiful Scenic Oklahoma in Photos

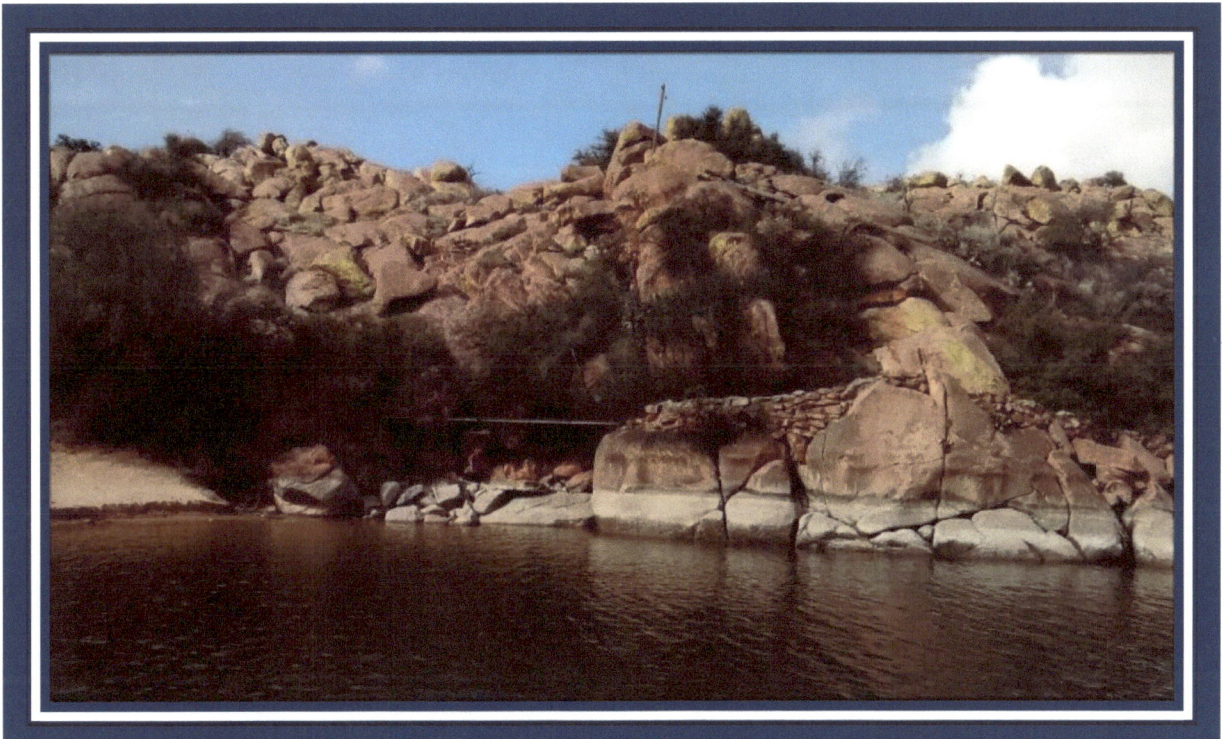

Beautiful Scenic Oklahoma in Photos

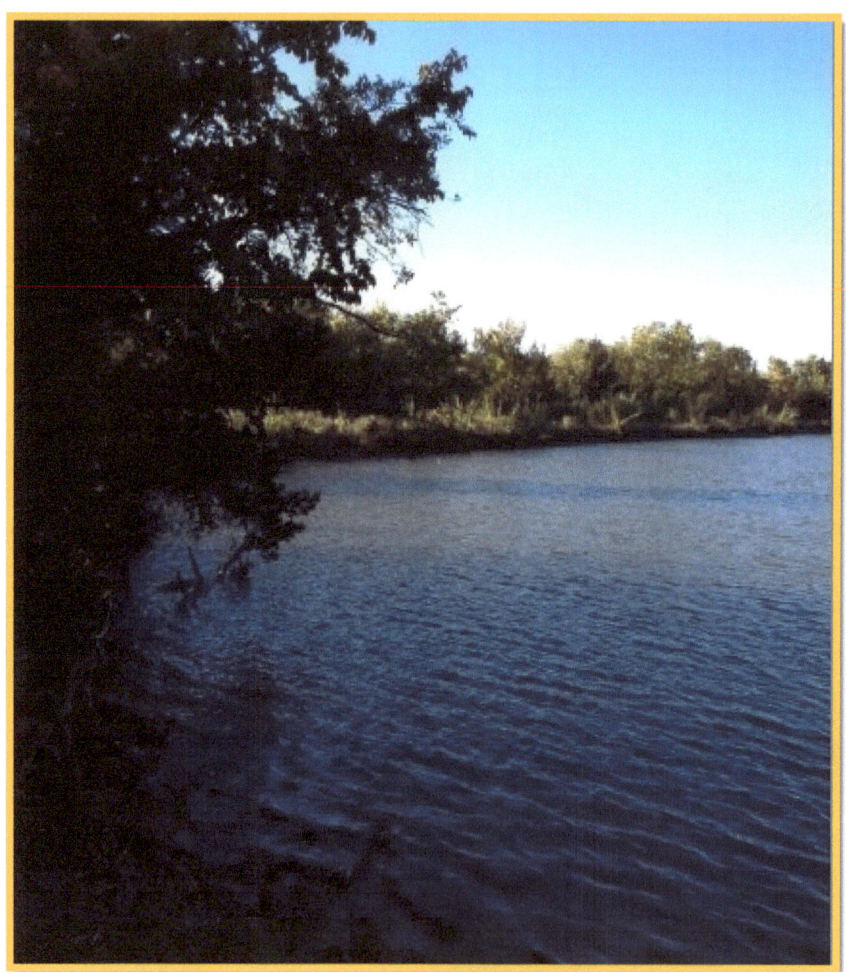

Beautiful Scenic Oklahoma in Photos

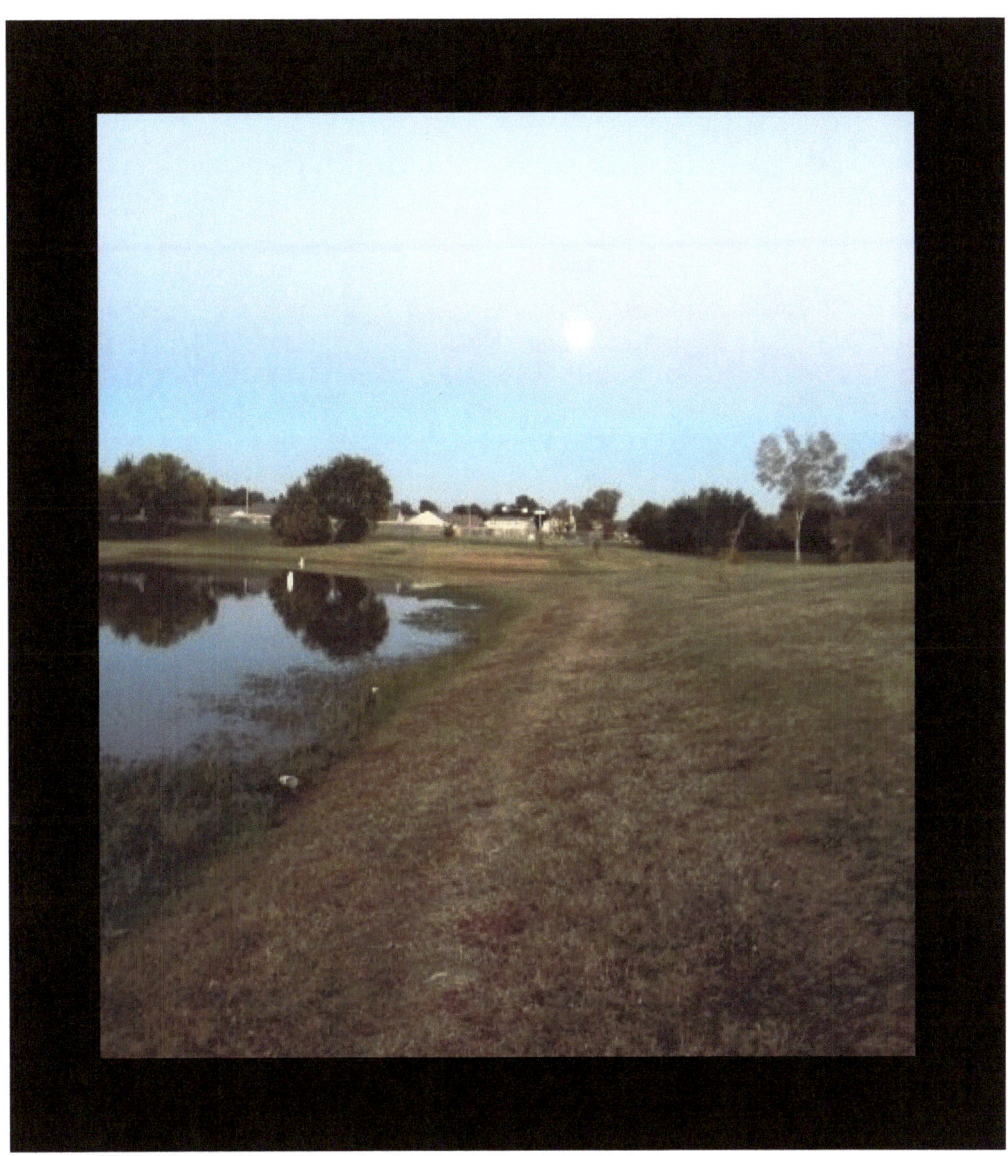

Beautiful Scenic Oklahoma in Photos

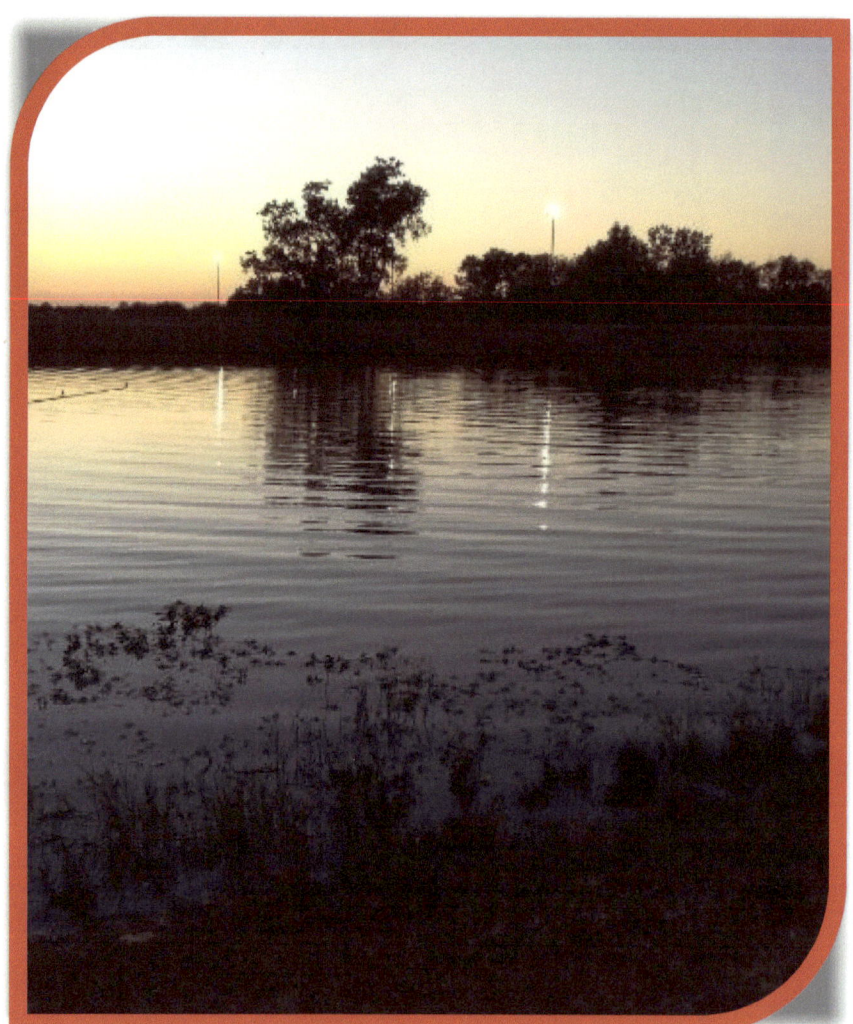

Beautiful Scenic Oklahoma in Photos

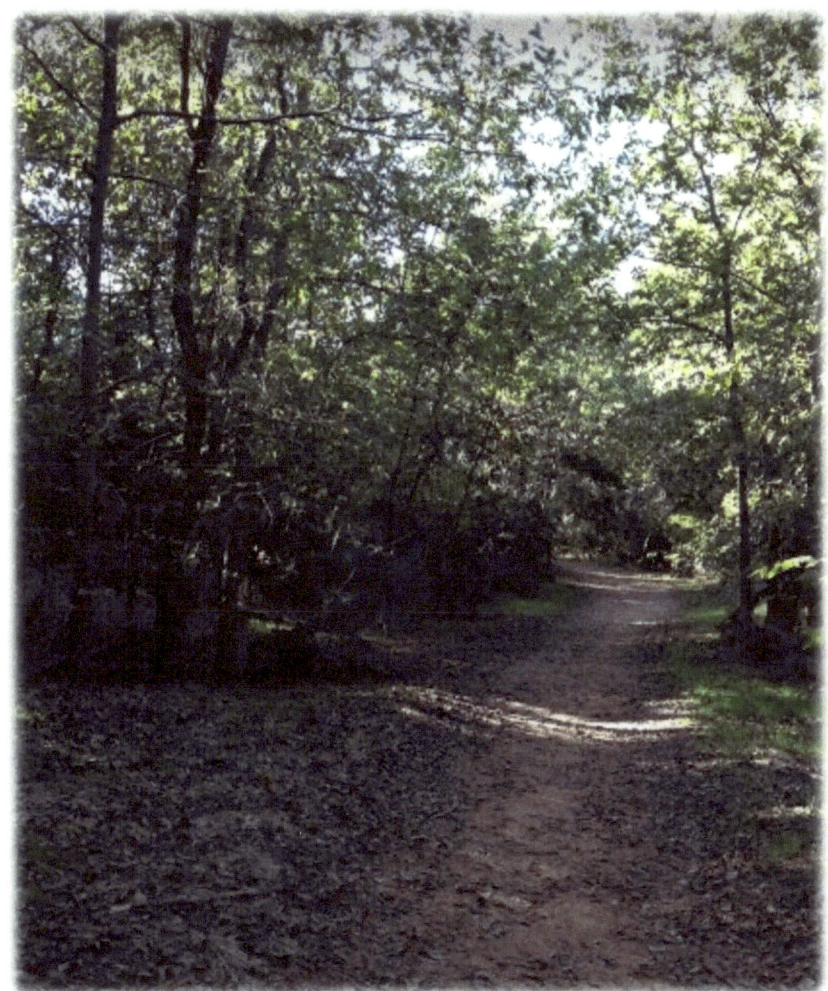

Beautiful Scenic Oklahoma in Photos

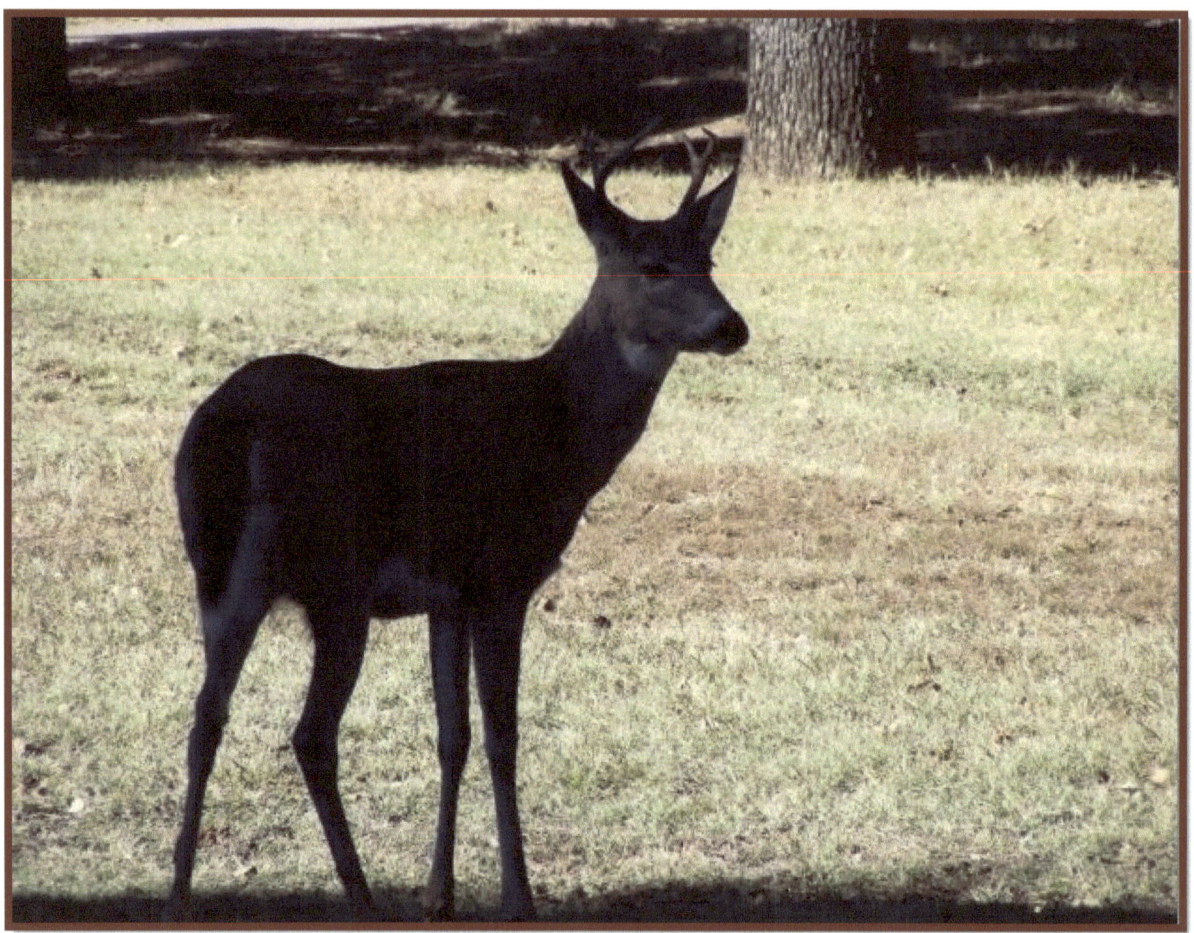

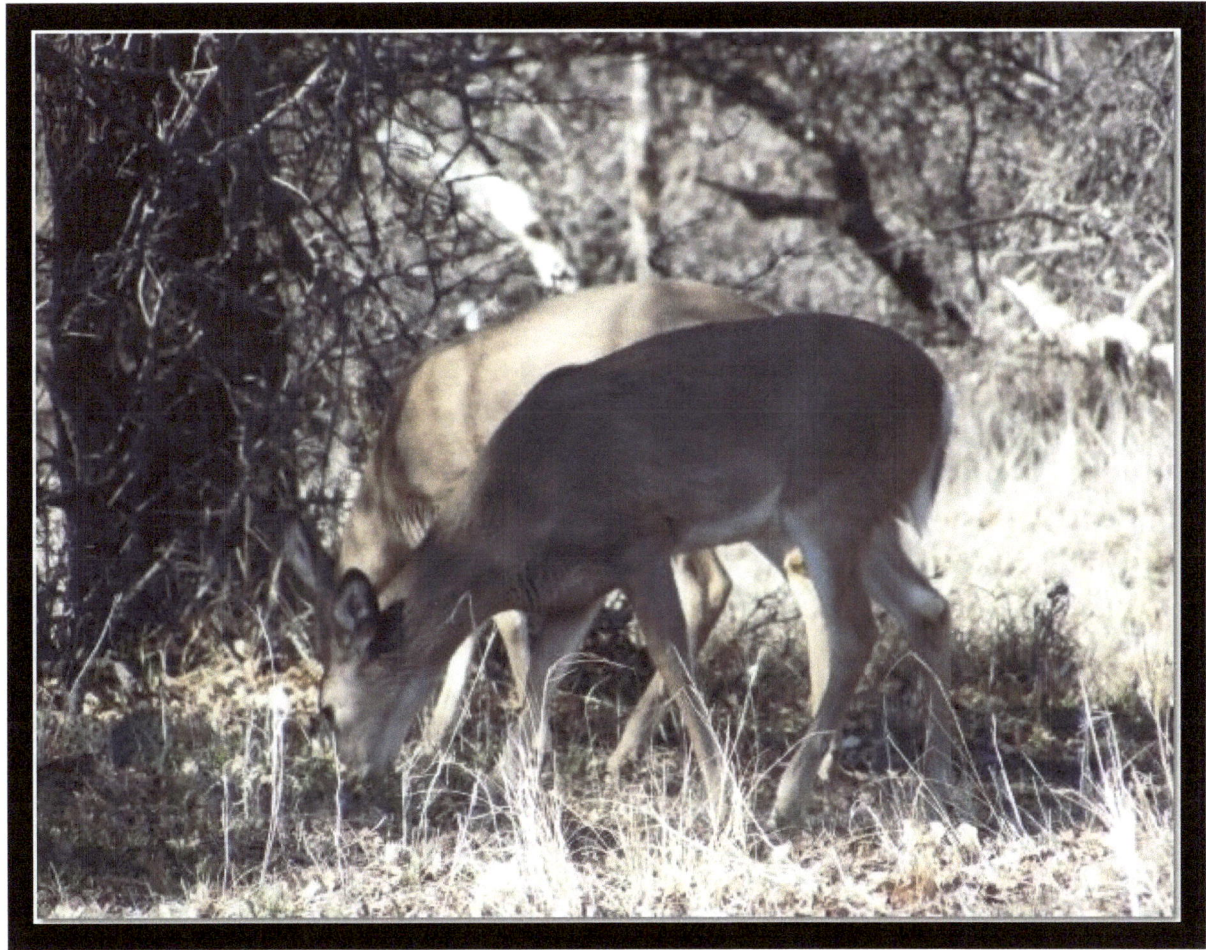

Beautiful Scenic Oklahoma in Photos

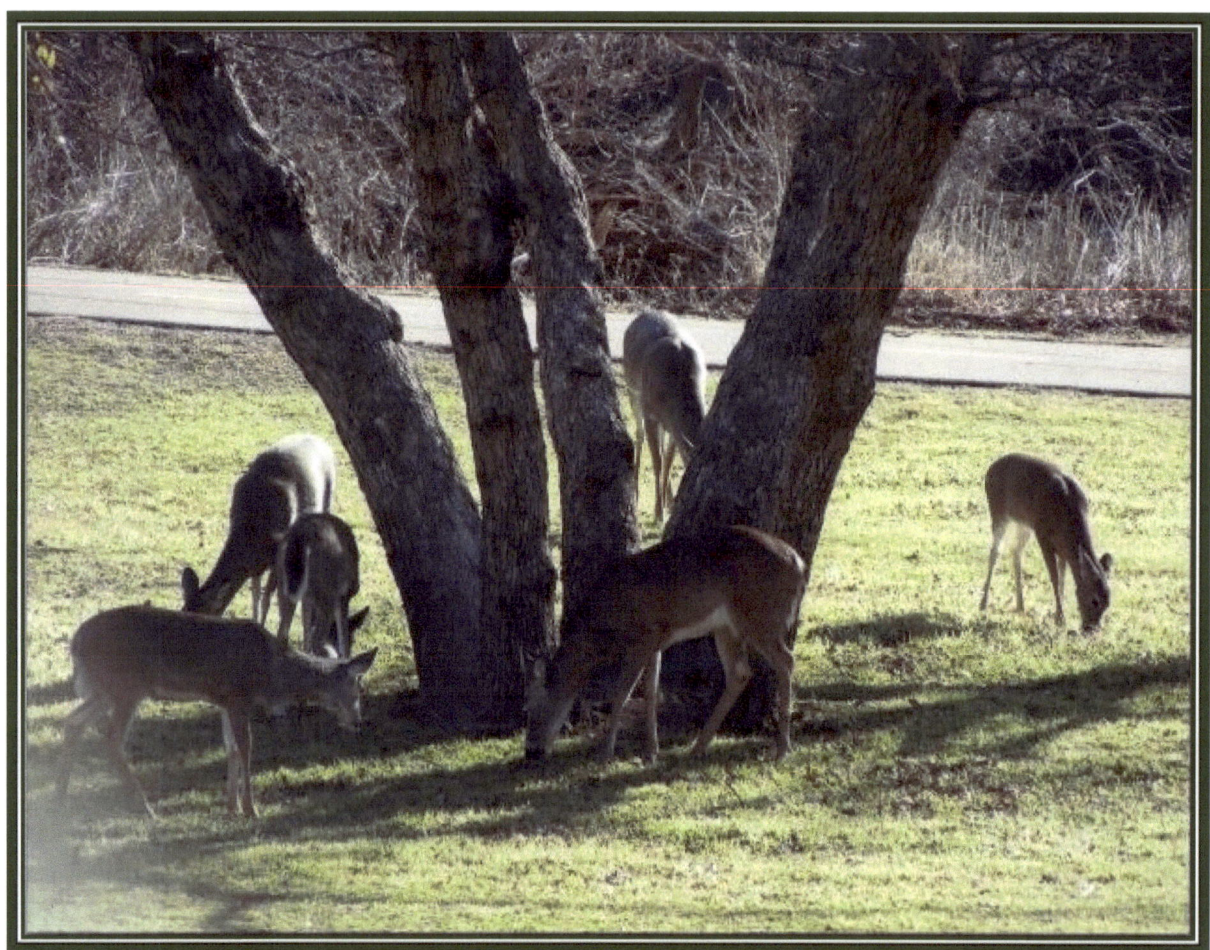

Beautiful Scenic Oklahoma in Photos

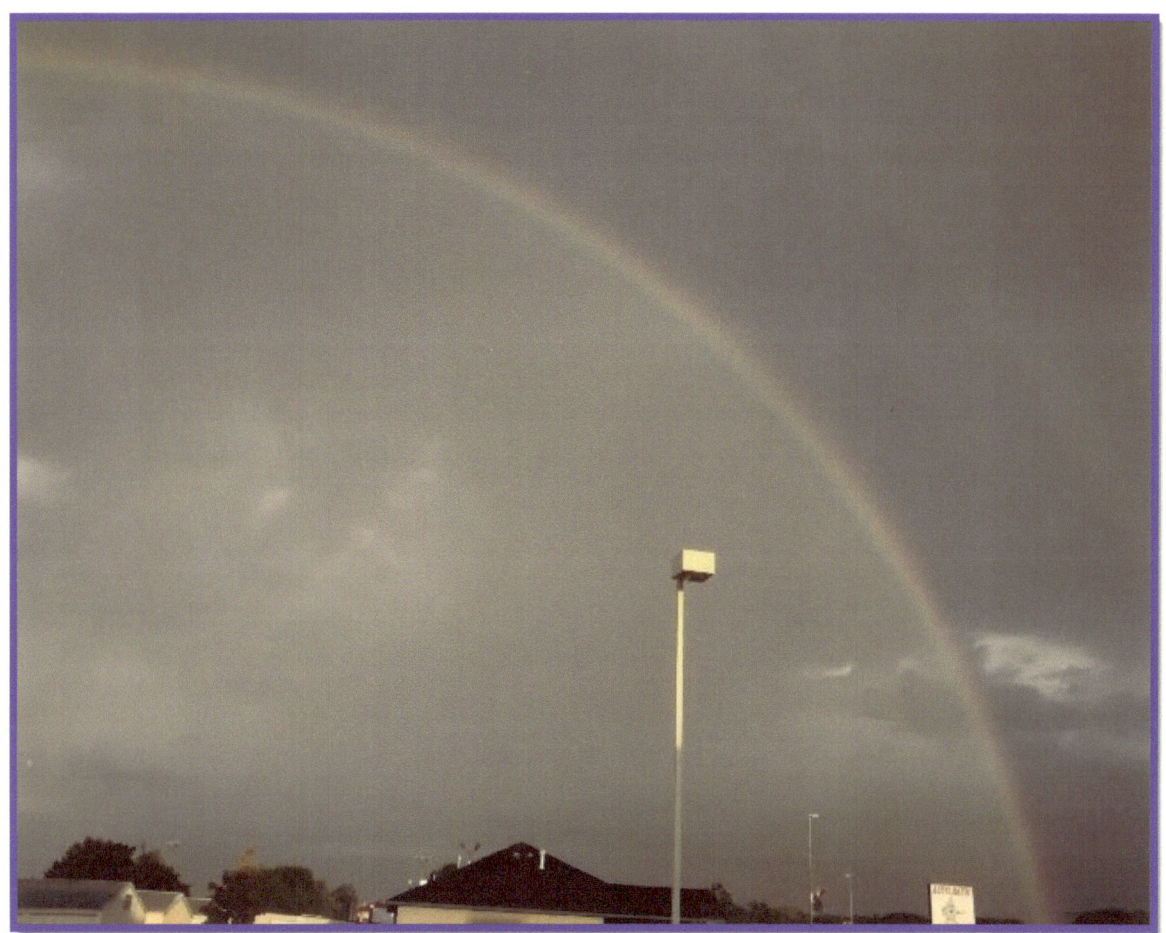

Beautiful Scenic Oklahoma in Photos

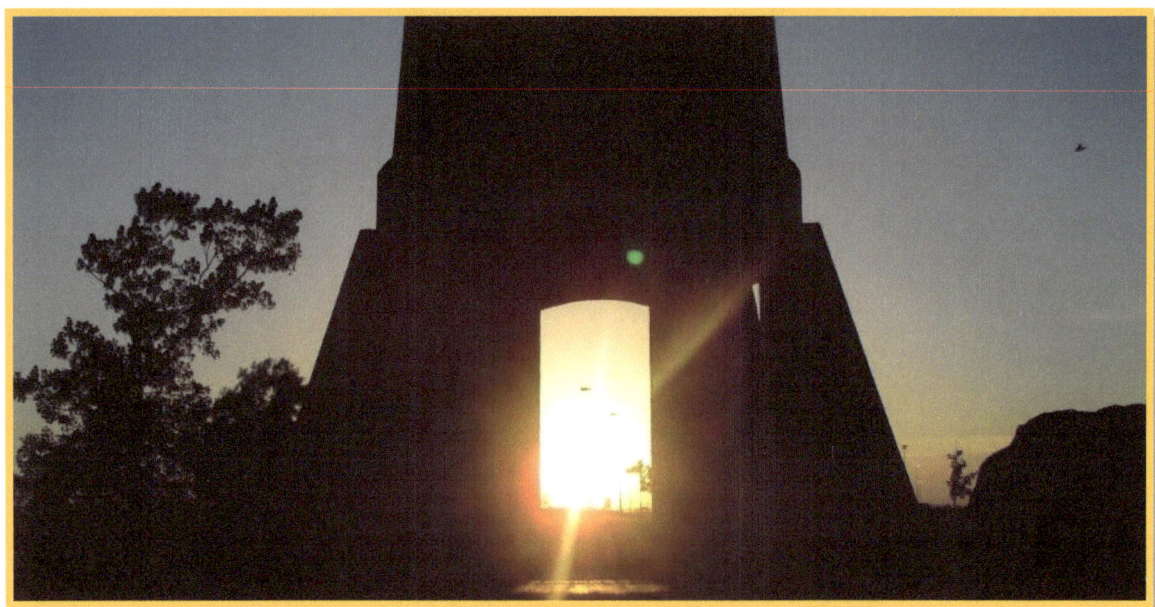

Beautiful Scenic Oklahoma in Photos

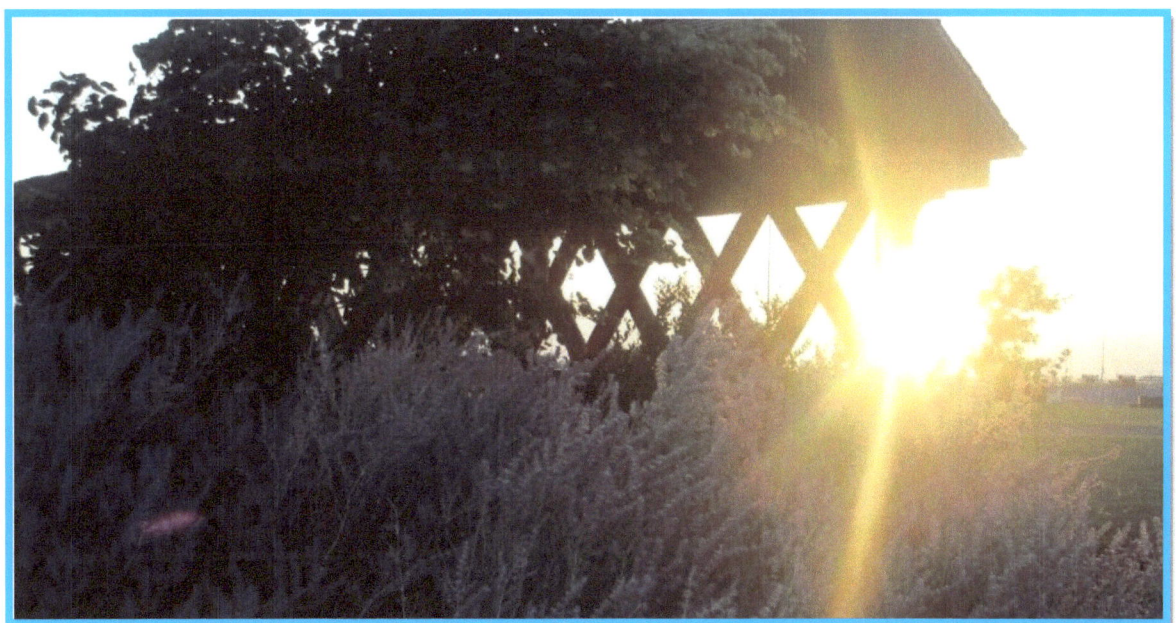

Beautiful Scenic Oklahoma in Photos

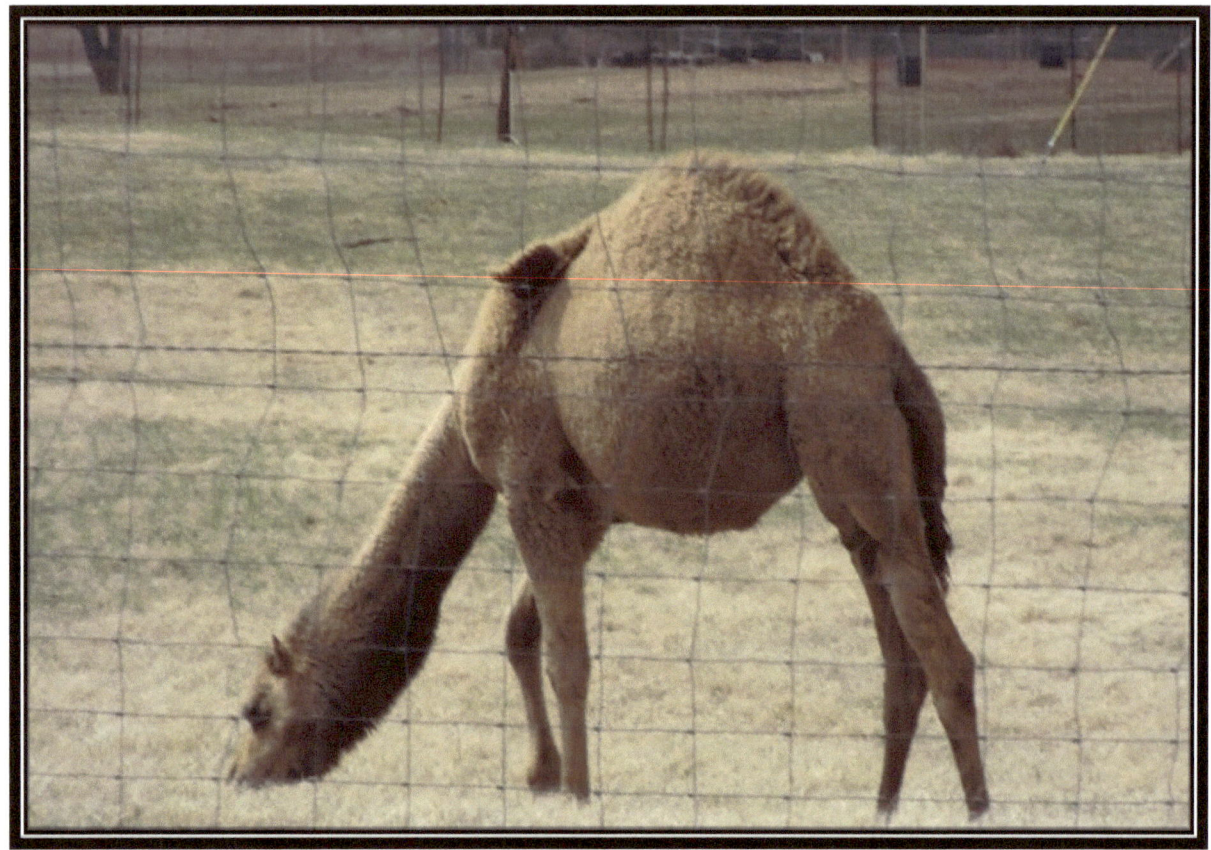

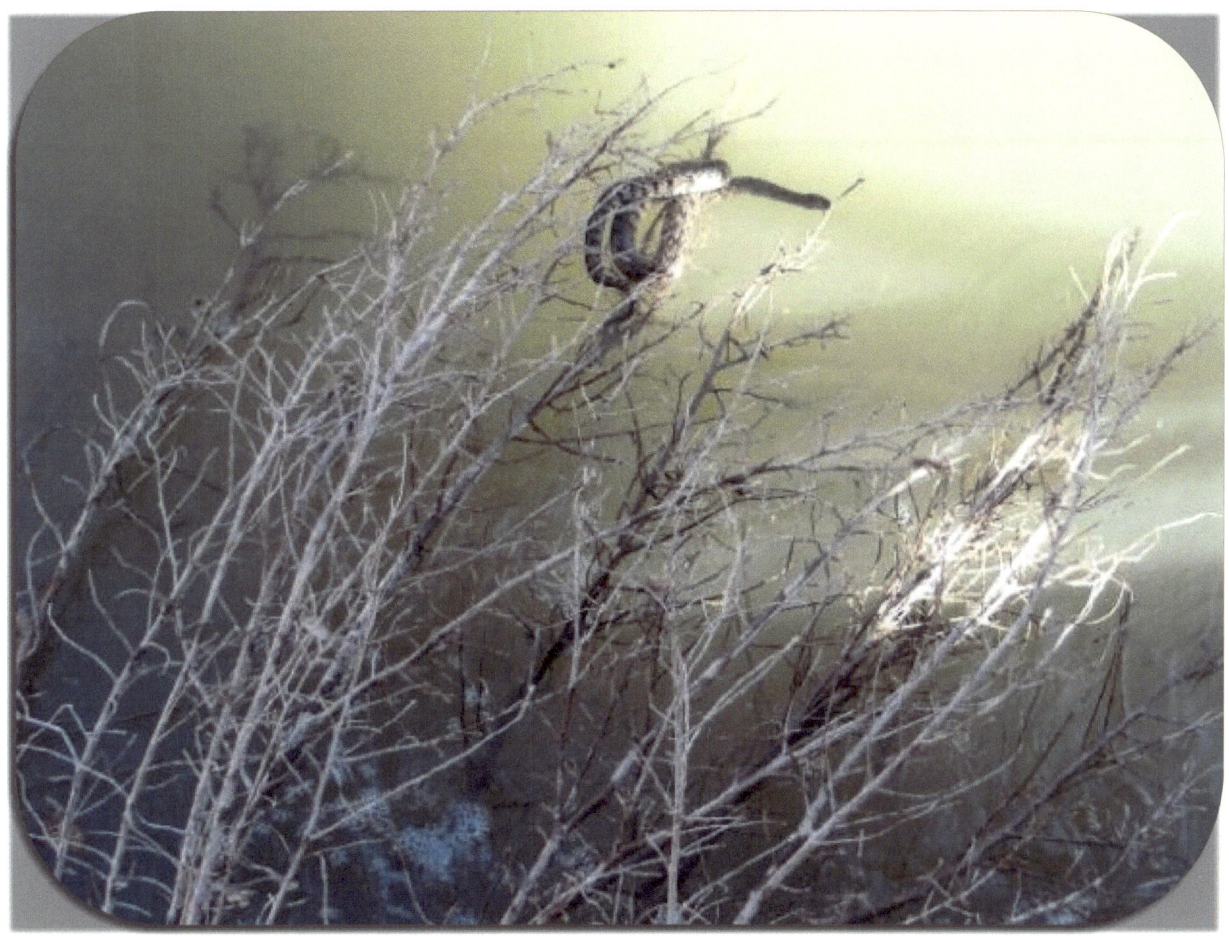

Beautiful Scenic Oklahoma in Photos

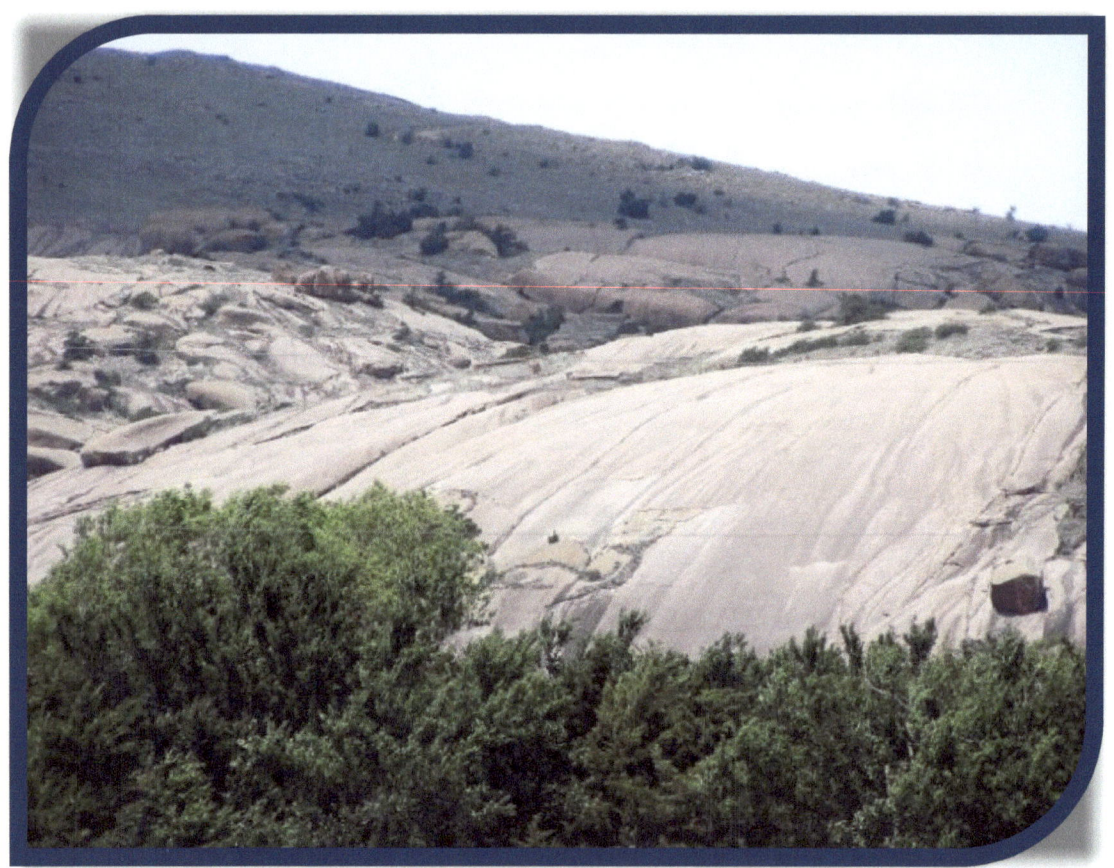

Beautiful Scenic Oklahoma in Photos

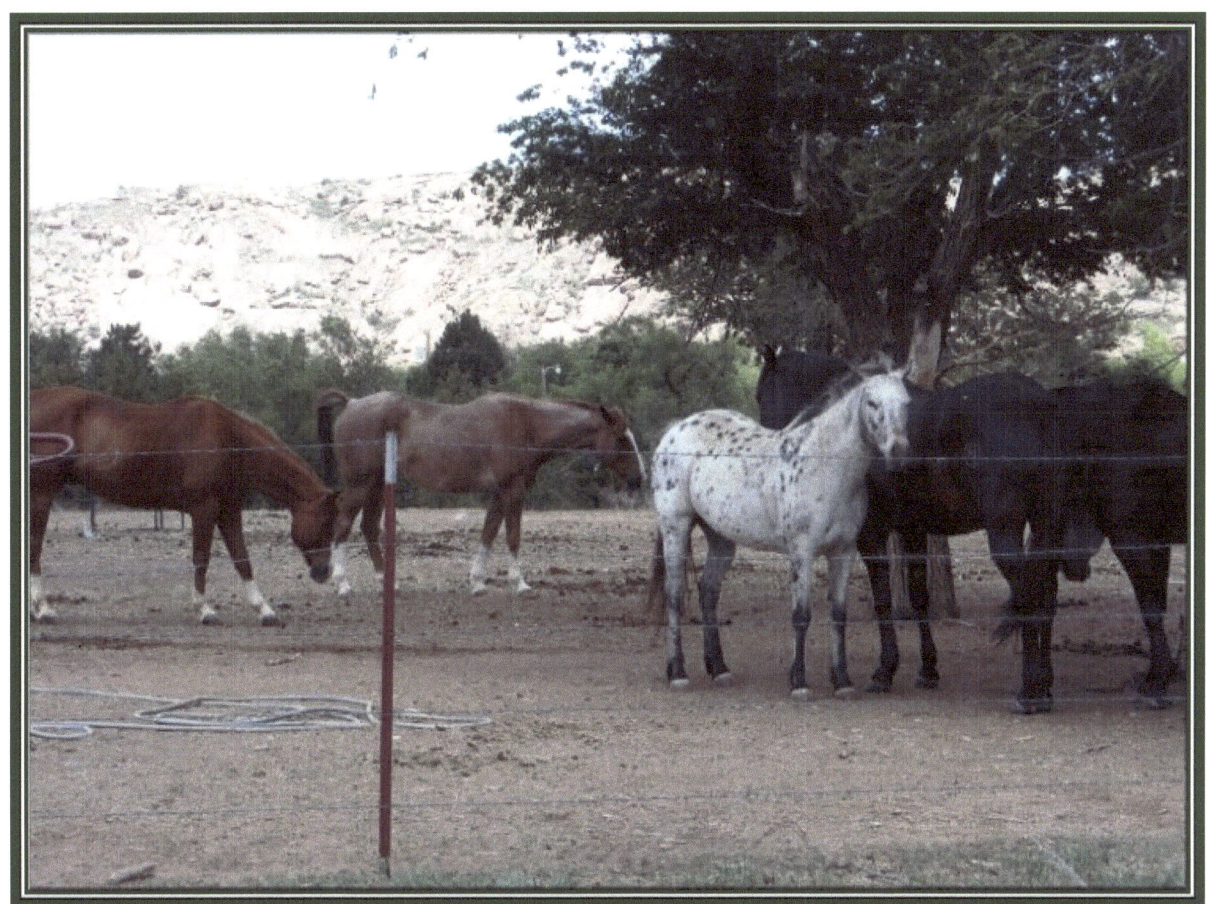

Beautiful Scenic Oklahoma in Photos

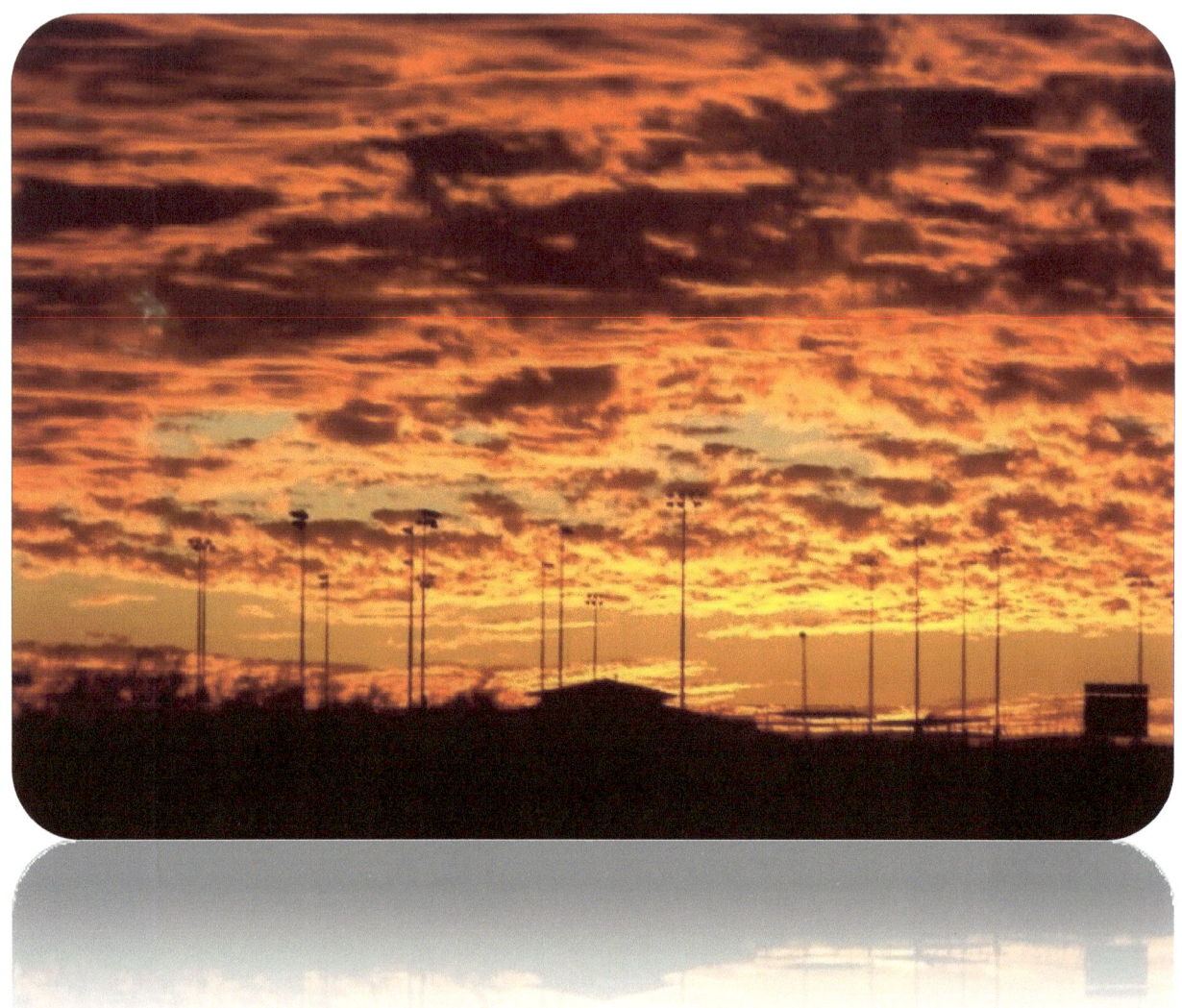

Beautiful Scenic Oklahoma in Photos

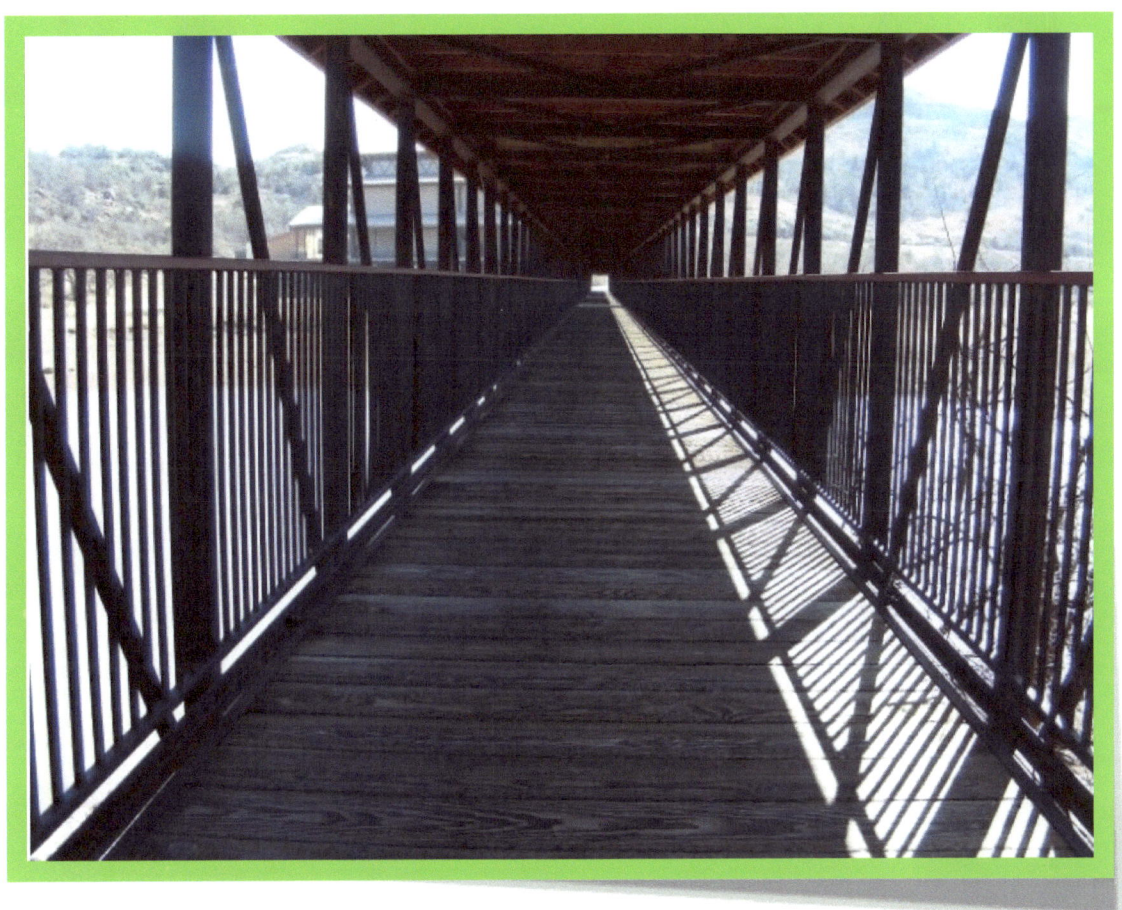

Beautiful Scenic Oklahoma in Photos

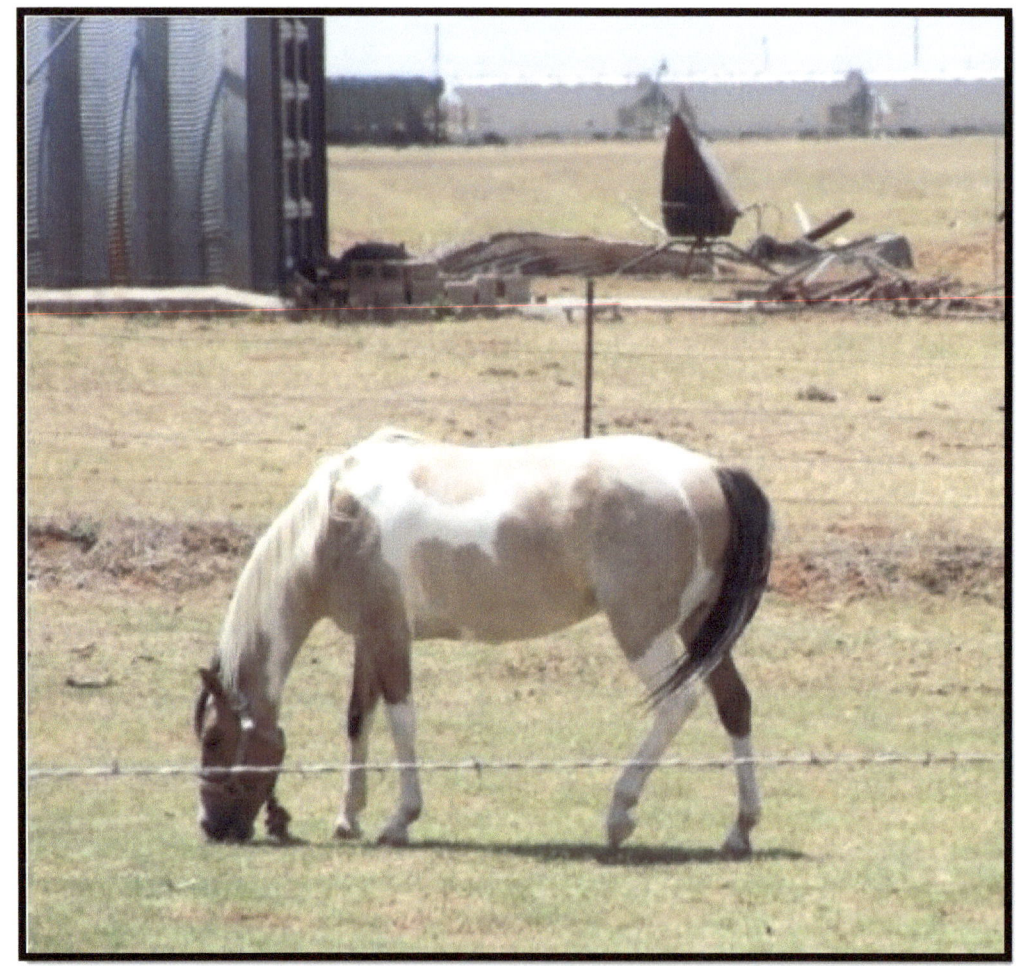

Beautiful Scenic Oklahoma in Photos

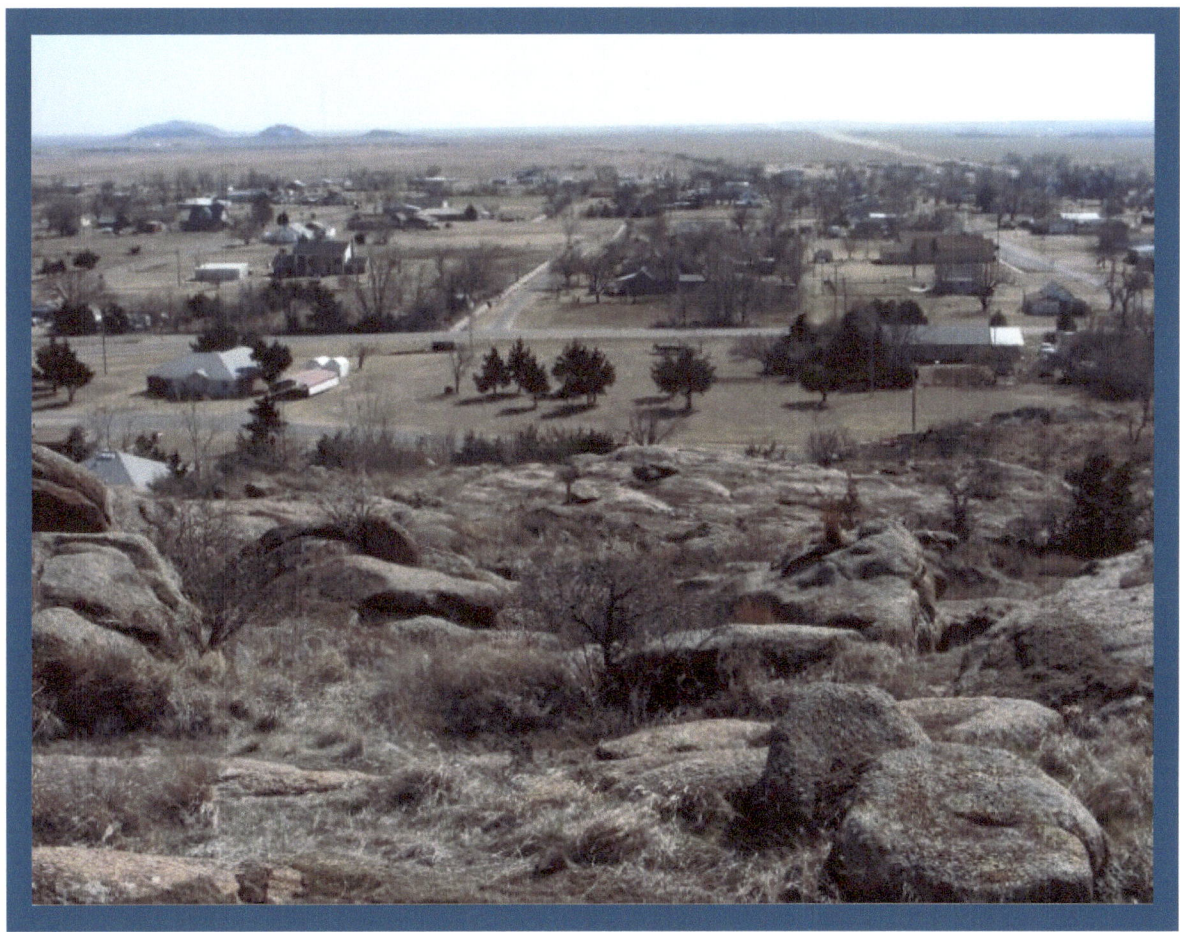

Beautiful Scenic Oklahoma in Photos

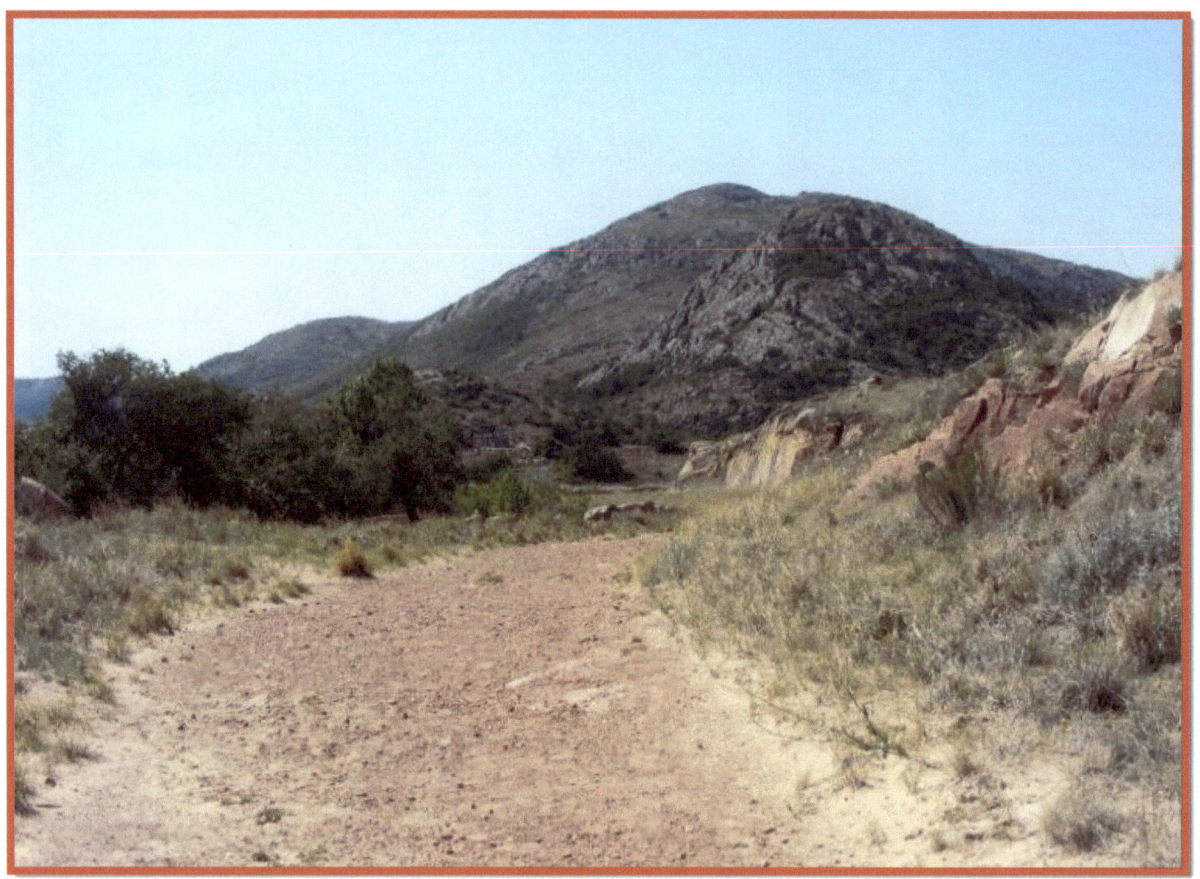

Beautiful Scenic Oklahoma in Photos

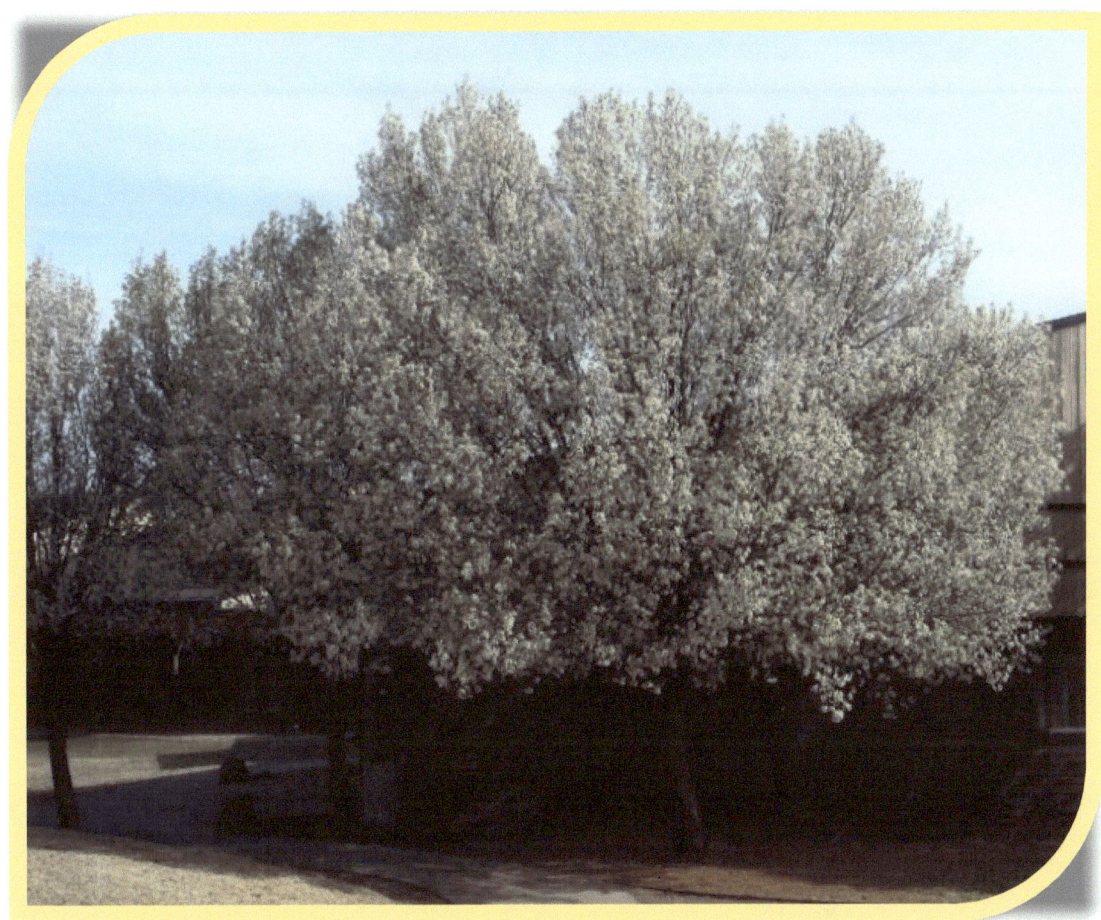

Beautiful Scenic Oklahoma in Photos

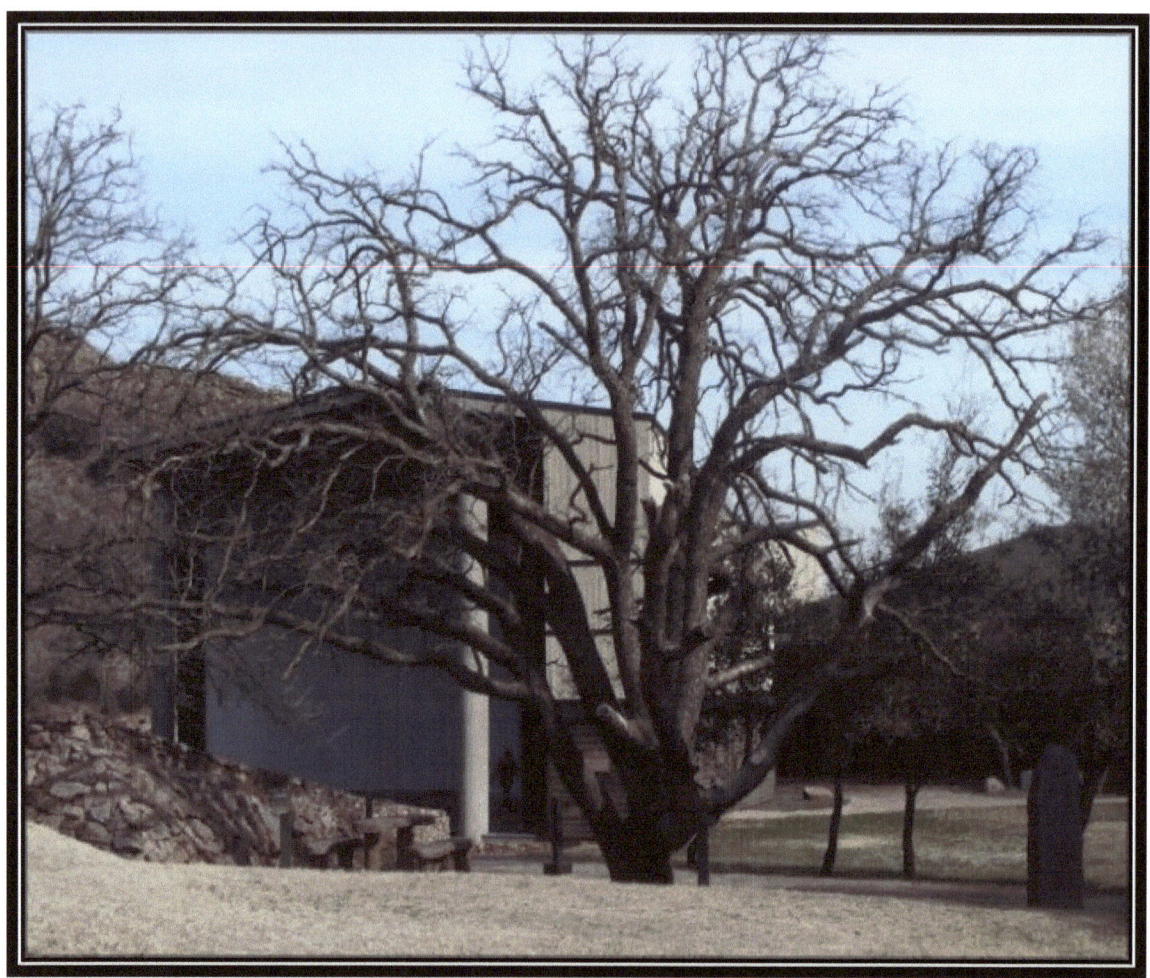

Beautiful Scenic Oklahoma in Photos

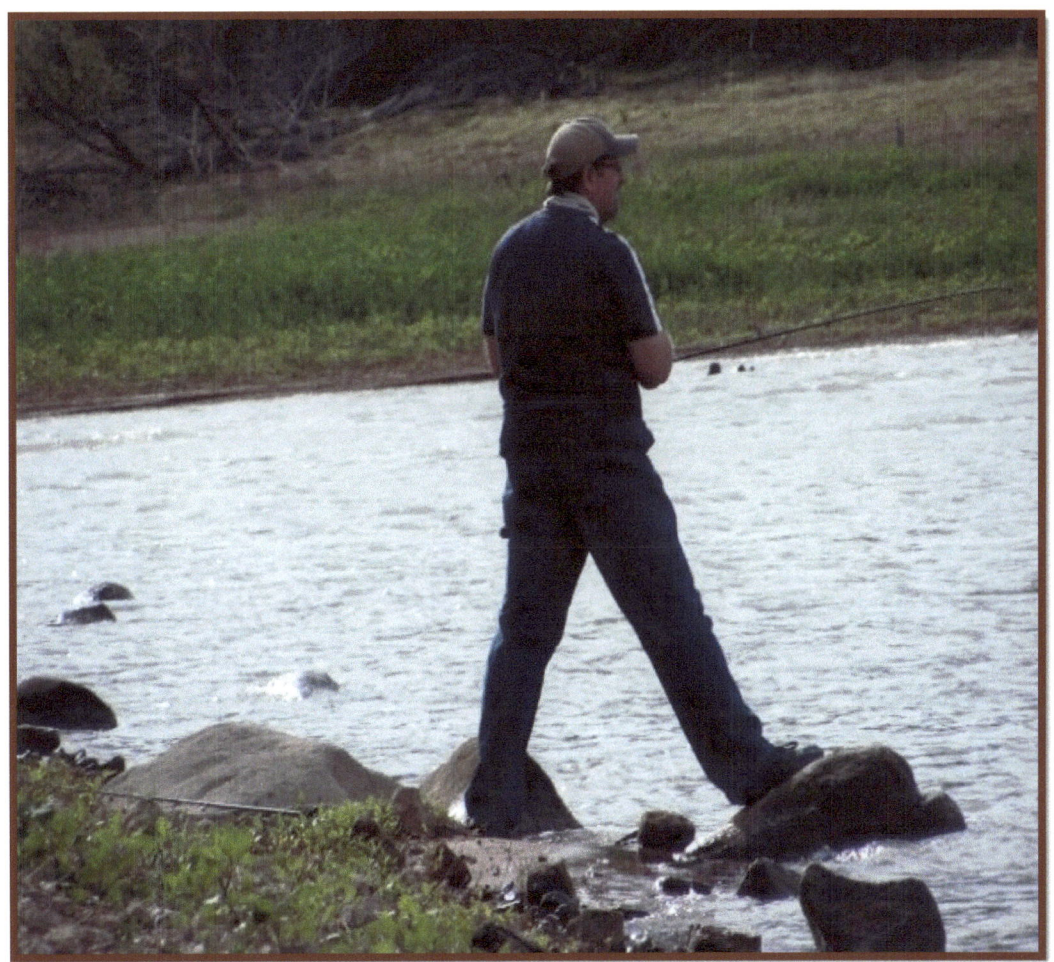

Beautiful Scenic Oklahoma in Photos

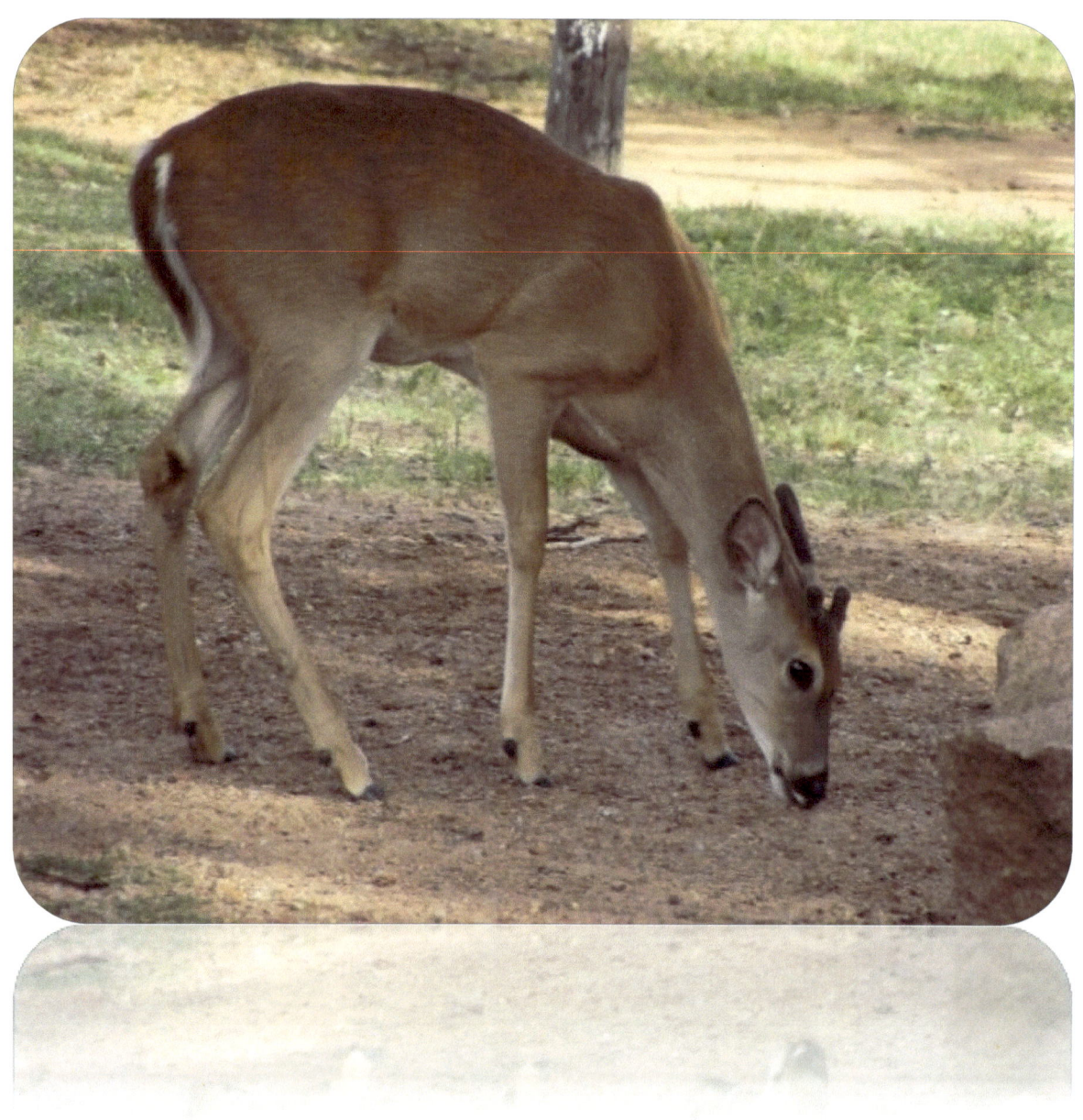

Beautiful Scenic Oklahoma in Photos

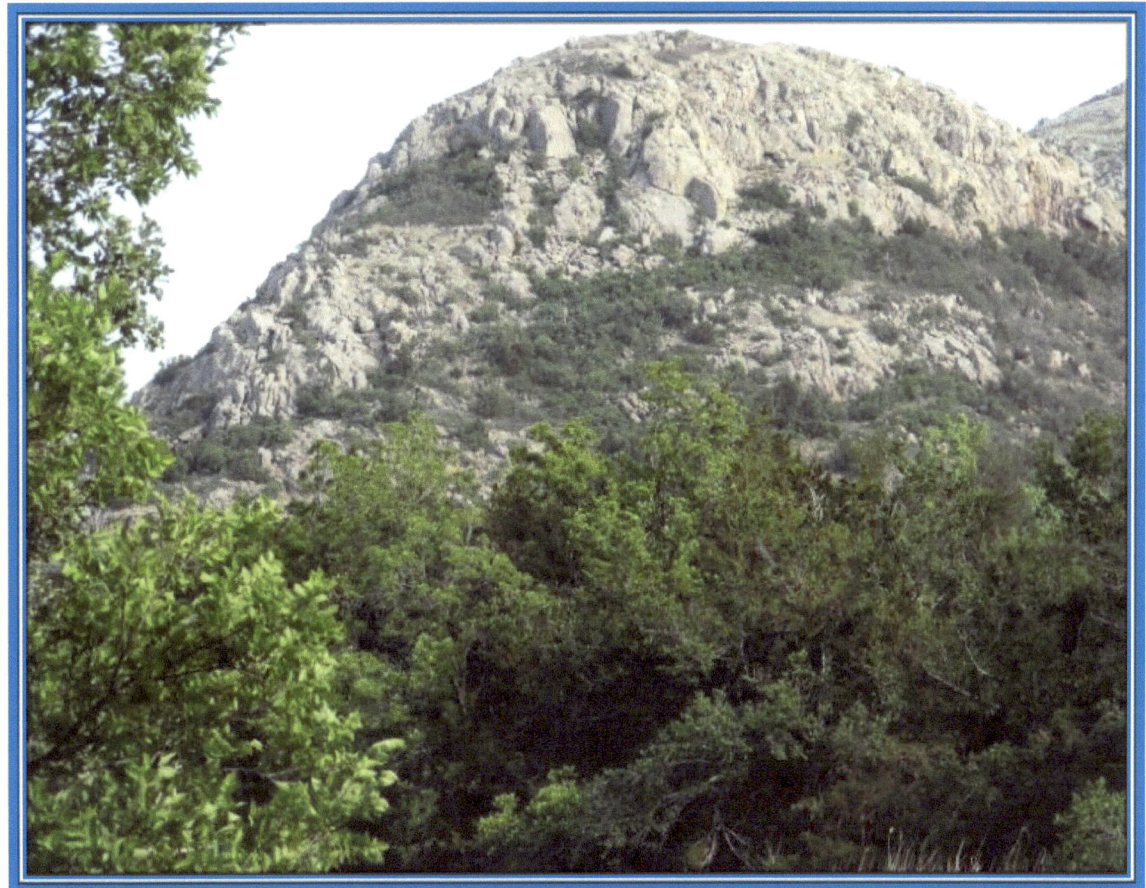

Beautiful Scenic Oklahoma in Photos

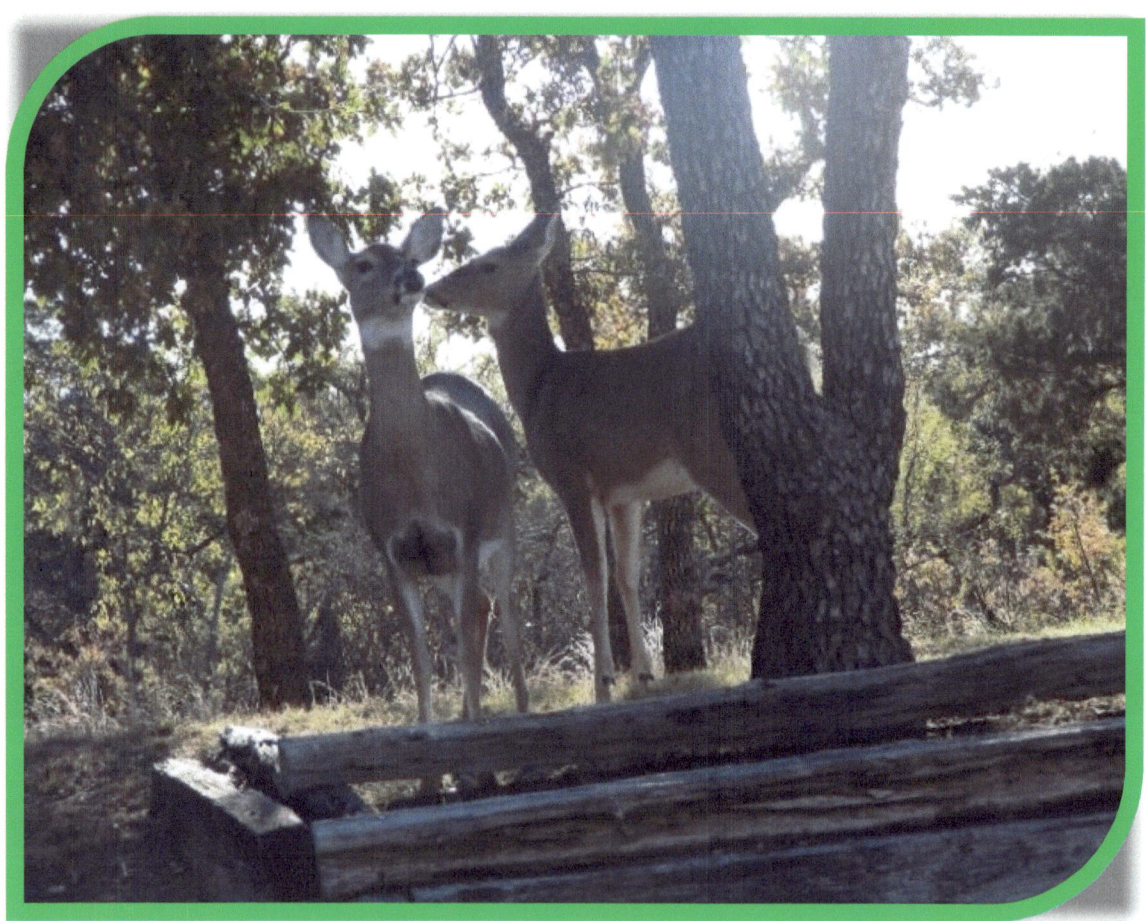

Beautiful Scenic Oklahoma in Photos

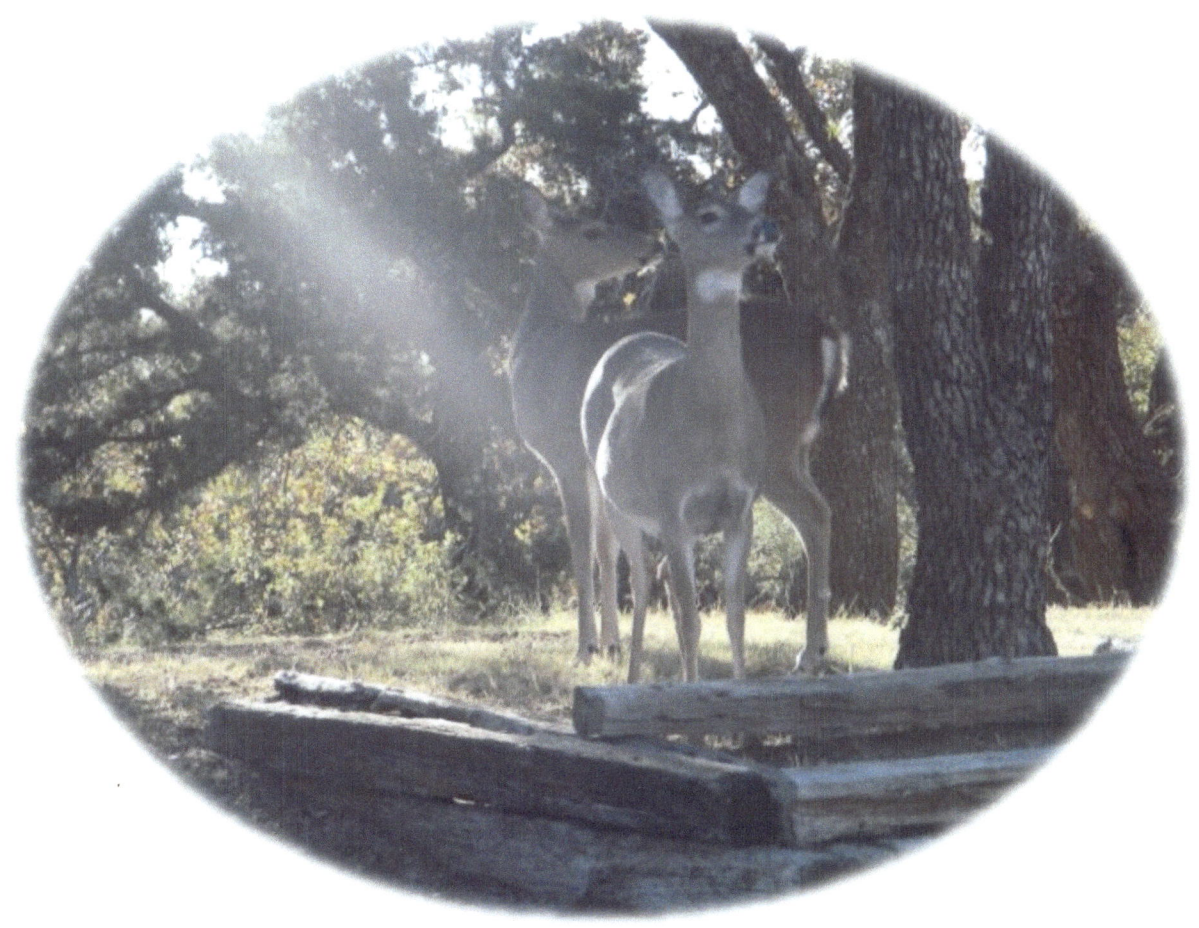

Beautiful Scenic Oklahoma in Photos

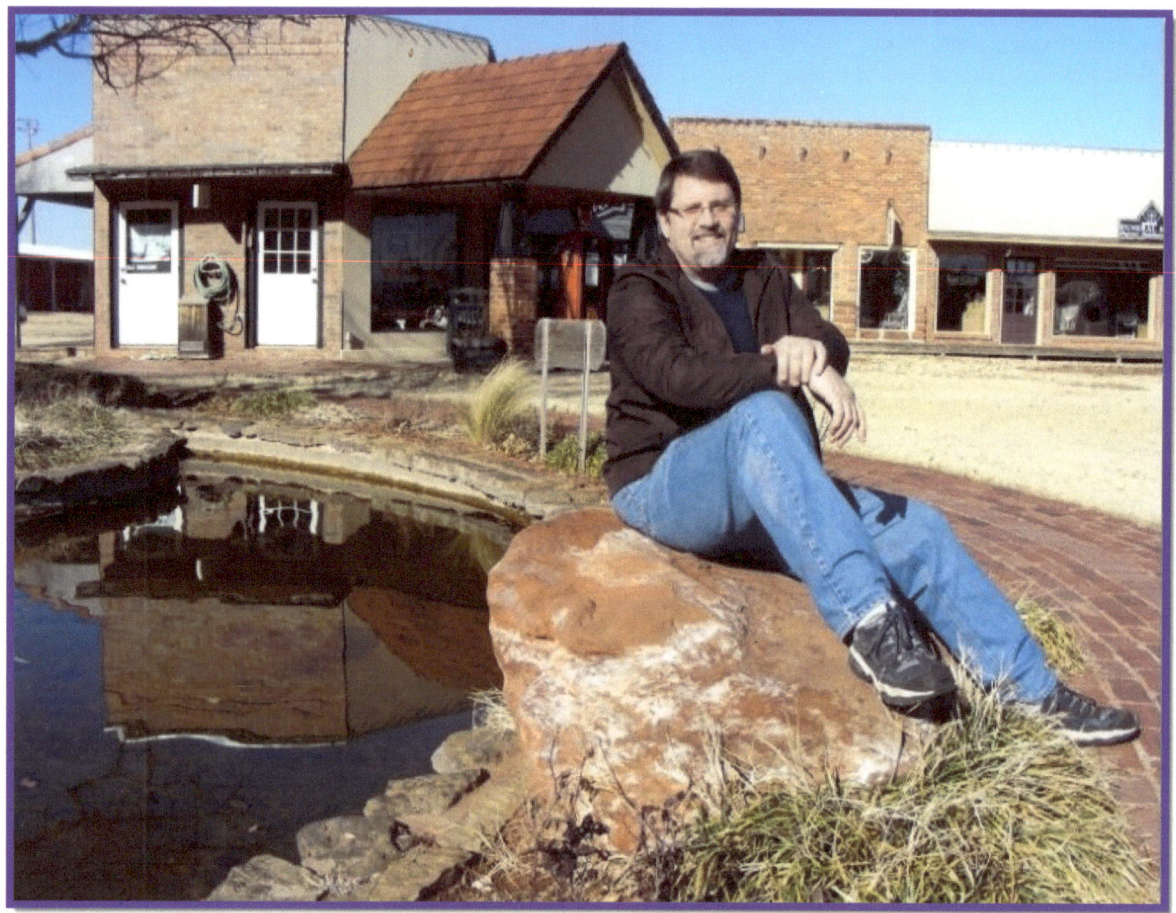

The Supportive husband and my best friend!

(END)